Hugo's Simplified System

Italian
Phrase Book

D0834952

Hugo's Language Books Limited

This revised edition
© 1993 Hugo's Language Books Ltd/Lexus Ltd
All rights reserved
ISBN 0 85285 202 9

2nd impression 1995

Compiled by
Lexus Ltd
with
Karen McAulay
and
Mariarosaria Cardines

This revised edition
compiled by
Lexus Ltd
with
Gabriella Bacchelli

*Facts and figures given in this book were
correct when printed. If you discover any
changes, please write to us.*

Set in 9/9 Plantin and Plantin Light by
Lexus Ltd with Dittoprint Ltd, Glasgow
Printed in Great Britain by
Page Bros, Norwich

CONTENTS

Preface	4
Introduction, Pronunciation	5
Useful Everyday Phrases	6
Colloquialisms	17
Days, Months, Seasons	18
Numbers	19
Time, The Calendar	20
Hotels	23
Camping and Caravanning	29
Villas and Apartments	32
Motoring	37
Travelling Around	45
Restaurants	58
Menu Guide	63
Shops and Services	79
Sport	90
Post Offices and Banks	96
Telephones	101
Emergencies	107
Health	113
Conversion Tables	120
Mini-Dictionary	121

PREFACE

This revised and enlarged edition is the latest in a long line of Hugo phrase books and is of excellent pedigree, having been compiled by experts to meet the general needs of tourists and business travellers. Arranged under the usual headings of 'Hotels', 'Motoring' and so forth, the ample selection of useful words and phrases is supported by a 2,000 line mini-dictionary. By cross-reference to this, scores of additional phrases may be formed. There is also an extensive menu guide listing approximately 600 dishes or methods of cooking and presentation.

Highlighted sections illustrate some of the replies you may be given and the signs or instructions you may see or hear. The pronunciation of words and phrases in the main text is imitated in English sound syllables, and particular characteristics of Italian are illustrated in the Introduction. You should have no difficulty managing the language, especially if you use our audio-cassette of selected extracts from the book. Ask your bookseller for the Hugo Italian Travel Pack.

INTRODUCTION

PRONUNCIATION

When reading the imitated pronunciation, stress that part which is underlined. Pronounce each syllable as if it formed part of an English word, and you will be understood sufficiently well. Remember the points below, and your pronunciation will be even closer to the correct Italian. Use our audio-cassette of selected extracts from this book, and you should be word-perfect!

ai as in 'fair'
ay as in 'pay'
e as in 'bed'
g always hard as in 'get'
I as in 'I'
ow as in 'cow'
r is always strongly pronounced
y always pronounced as in 'yet' except in 'ay' as above

Note that when there are two identical consonants separated by a hyphen, eg **vorrei** – *vor-ray*, both consonants must be pronounced as if you were pronouncing two separate English words: eg **jus̲t̲ two**, **ful̲l̲ length**.

GENDERS AND ARTICLES

Italian has two genders for nouns – masculine and feminine. In the vocabulary section of this book, we generally give the definite article ('the'). For masculine nouns, the definite article is **il** (plural **i**) before nouns beginning with a consonant; **lo** (plural **gli**) before nouns beginning with 's' + consonant or 'z'; and **l'** (plural **gli**) before nouns beginning with a vowel. For feminine nouns, use **la** before a noun beginning with a consonant and **l'** before a vowel (plural **le**).

The masculine indefinite article ('a') is **uno** before a noun beginning with a consonant and **un** before a vowel. The feminine is **una** before a consonant and **un'** before a vowel.

USEFUL EVERYDAY PHRASES

YES, NO, OK ETC

Yes/No
Sì/No
see/no

Excellent!
Ottimo!
ot-teemo

Don't!
Non farlo!
non farlo

OK
OK
'ok'

That's fine
Va bene
va baynay

That's right
È vero
eh vayro

GREETINGS, INTRODUCTIONS

How do you do, pleased to meet you
Piacere di conoscerla
pee-achairay dee konoshairla

Good morning/Good evening/Good night
Buon giorno/Buona sera/Buona notte
bwon jorno/bwona saira/bwona not-tay

Goodbye
Arrivederci
ar-reevedairchee

How are you?　　　　*(familiar)*
Come sta?　　　　　　Come stai?
komay sta　　　　　　*komay stı*

My name is ...
Mi chiamo...
mee k-yamo

What's your name?　　*(familiar)*
Come si chiama?　　　　Come ti chiami?
komay see k-yama　　　*komay tee k-yamee*

What's his/her name?
Come si chiama?
komay see k-yama

May I introduce ...?
Posso presentarle...?
pos-so prezentarlay

This is ... *(introducing male/female)*
Questo è.../Questa è...
kwesto eh/kwesta eh

Hello
Ciao
chow

Hi!
Salve!
salvay

Bye!/Cheerio!
Ciao!
chow

7

See you later
A più tardi
a p-yoo tardee

It's been nice meeting you
Mi ha fatto piacere conoscerla
mee a fat-to pee-achairay konoshairla

PLEASE, THANK YOU, APOLOGIES

Thank you/No thank you
Grazie/No grazie
gratzee-ay/no gratzee-ay

Yes please
Sì grazie
see gratzee-ay

Please *(offering)*   *(asking for something)*
Prego   Per favore/per piacere
praygo   *pair favoray/pair pee-achairay*

Excuse me! *(when belching/sneezing etc)*
Scusate!
skoozatay

Sorry!   *(familiar)*
Scusi!   Scusa!
skoozee   *skooza*

I'm really sorry
Sono davvero spiacente
sono dav-vairo spee-achentay

It was/wasn't my fault!
È/non è stata colpa mia!
eh/non eh stata kolpa mee-a

WHERE, HOW, ASKING

Excuse me please *(to get past etc)*
Permesso
pairmesso

Can you tell me …?
Potrebbe dirmi...?
potrayb-bay deermee

Can I have …?
Potrei avere...?
potray avairay

Would you like a …?
Vorrebbe un/una...?
vor-rayb-bay oon/oona

Would you like to …?
Le piacerebbe...?
lay pee-achairayb-bay

Is there … here?
C'è...?
cheh

What's that?
Che cos'è?
kay kozeh

Where can I get …?
Dove potrei trovare...?
dovay potray trovaray

How much is it?
Quanto costa?
kwanto kosta

Where is the ...?
Dov'è il/la...?
dov<u>eh</u> eel/la

Where are the toilets, please?
Per cortesia, dove sono i servizi?
pair kortayz<u>ee</u>-a d<u>o</u>vay s<u>o</u>no ee sairv<u>ee</u>tzee

ABOUT ONESELF

I'm from ...
Sono di...
s<u>o</u>no dee

I'm ... years old
Ho... anni
oh ... <u>a</u>n-nee

I'm a ... *(occupation)*
Faccio il/la...
f<u>a</u>cho eel/la

I'm married/single/divorced *(said by a man)*
Sono sposato/celibe/divorziato
s<u>o</u>no spoz<u>a</u>to/ch<u>e</u>leebay/deevortz-y<u>a</u>to

(said by a woman)
Sono sposata/nubile/divorziata
s<u>o</u>no spoz<u>a</u>ta/n<u>oo</u>beelay/deevortz-y<u>a</u>ta

I have ... sisters/brothers/children
Ho... sorelle/fratelli/bambini
oh ... sor<u>e</u>l-lay/frat<u>e</u>l-lee/bamb<u>ee</u>nee

LIKES, DISLIKES, SOCIALIZING

I like/love ...
Mi piace...
mee pee-<u>a</u>chay

I don't like ...
Non mi piace...
non mee pee-achay

I like swimming/travelling
Mi piace nuotare/viaggiare
mee pee-achay nwotaray/vyaj-jaray

I hate ...
Odio...
odee-o

Do you like ...?
Le piace...?
lay pee-achay

It's delicious/awful!
È buonissimo/terribile!
eh bwonees-seemo/ter-reebeelay

I don't drink/smoke
Non bevo/fumo
non bayvo/foomo

Do you mind if I smoke?
Le dispiace se fumo?
lay deespee-achay say foomo

I don't eat meat or fish
Non mangio nè la carne nè il pesce
non manjo neh la karnay neh eel peshay

What would you like (to drink)?
Cosa desidera (da bere)?
koza dezeedaira da bairay

I would like a ...
Vorrei un/una...
vor-ray oon/oona

11

Nothing for me thanks
Per me niente, grazie
pair may nee-entay gratzee-ay

I'll get this one
Prenderò questo
prendairo kwesto

Cheers! *(toast)*
Alla salute!/Cin cin!
al-la salootay/cheen cheen

I would like to ...
Vorrei...
vor-ray

Let's go to Florence/the cinema/the exhibition
Andiamo a Firenze/al cinema/alla mostra
and-yamo a feerentzay/al cheenema/al-la mostra

Let's go swimming/for a walk
Andiamo a nuotare/a fare una passeggiata
and-yamo a nwotaray/a faray oona pas-sej-jata

What's the weather like?
Che tempo fa?
kay tempo fa

The weather's awful
È brutto tempo
eh broot-to tempo

It's pouring down
Sta piovendo a dirotto
sta p-yovendo a deerot-to

It's really hot
Fa veramente caldo
fa veramentay kaldo

It's sunny
C'è il sole
cheh eel solay

HELP, PROBLEMS

Can you help me?
Può aiutarmi?
pwo I-ootarmee

I don't understand
Non capisco
non kapeesko

Do you speak English/French/German?
Parla inglese/francese/tedesco?
parla eenglayzay/franchayzay/tedesko

Does anyone here speak English?
C'è qualcuno che parla inglese?
cheh kwalkoono kay parla eenglayzay

I can't speak Italian
Non parlo italiano
non parlo eetal-yano

I don't know
Non so
non so

What's wrong?
Cosa c'è che non va?
koza cheh kay non va

Please speak more slowly
Per favore, parli più lentamente
pair favoray parlee p-yoo lentamentay

13

Please write it down for me
Me lo scriva, per favore
may lo skreeva pair favoray

I've lost my way *(said by a man/woman)*
Mi sono perso/persa
mee sono pairso/pairsa

Go away!   *(familiar)*
Se ne vada!   Vattene!
say nay vada   *vat-tenay*

TALKING TO RECEPTIONISTS ETC

I have an appointment with ...
Ho un appuntamento con...
oh oon ap-poontamento kon

I'd like to see ...
Vorrei vedere...
vor-ray vedairay

Here's my card
Questo è il mio biglietto da visita
kwesto eh eel mee-o beel-yet-to da veez-eeta

My company is ...
La mia società è...
la mee-a socheta eh

May I use your phone?
Posso usare il telefono?
pos-so oozaray eel telefono

THINGS YOU'LL SEE

affittasi	to let
aperto	open

→

acqua potabile	drinking water
ascensore	lift
buffet	snack bar
cassa	till, cash point
chiuso	closed
chiuso per ferie	closed for holiday period
entrata	way in, entrance
entrata libera	admission free
feriali	working days
festivi	public holidays
gabinetti	toilets
libero	vacant, free
occupato	engaged
orario di apertura	opening hours
orario di visita	visiting hours
piano terra	ground floor
primo piano	first floor
riservato	reserved
saldi/sconti	sales
servizi	toilets
signore	ladies
signori	gents
si prega di non...	please do not ...
spingere	push
strada	road
svendita	sale
tirare	pull
ufficio informazioni	tourist information
uscita	exit, way out
uscita di sicurezza	emergency exit
vendesi	for sale
vernice fresca	wet paint
via	street
vietato	forbidden
vietato l'ingresso	no admittance

THINGS YOU'LL HEAR

a più tardi	see you later
arrivederci	goodbye
attenzione!	look out!, attention!
avanti!	come in!
bene	good, fine
buon viaggio!	have a good trip!
ciao!	hello!; cheerio!
come, scusi?	pardon?
come stai/sta/state?	how are you?
come va?	how are things?
cosa hai/ha detto?	what did you say?
davvero?	really?
ecco qua!	here you are!
esattamente	exactly
grazie	thanks
grazie, anche a lei	thank you, the same to you
grazie molte	thank you very much
mi dispiace tanto!	I'm so sorry!
mi scusi	excuse me
molto bene, grazie	very well, thank you
– e lei?	– and you?
non capisco	I don't understand
non so	I don't know
piacere di conoscerla	how do you do, nice to meet you
prego	you're welcome, don't mention it; please
prego?	pardon?
salve!	hi!
serviti/si serva/servitevi	help yourself
sì	yes
va bene	that's right

COLLOQUIALISMS

You may hear these: to use some of them yourself could be risky!

accidenti!	damn!
che schifo!	it's disgusting!
chiudi il becco!	shut up!
cretino	idiot, fool
Dio mio!	my God!
e allora?	so what?
è orribile!	it's awful!
fa' pure!	do as you please!, please, do!
grazie a Dio!	thank God!
maledetto...	cursed ...
maledizione!	damn!
ma va?	really?
ma va!	I don't believe it
meglio così	so much the better
merda!	shit!
muoviti!	hurry up!
non posso crederci!	I can't believe it!
occhio!	watch out!
per Dio!	by God!
porca miseria!	bloody hell!
prova!	just try!
sei pazzo?	you must be crazy!
sparisci!	scram!
stupendo!	brilliant!
svitato	cracked, nutty
ti sta bene!	it serves you right!
tizio	bloke
togliti dai piedi!	get out of the way!
va al diavolo!/va all'inferno!	go to hell!
va a quel paese!	get lost!
va bene!	that's fine!, it's OK!
zitto!	shut up!

DAYS, MONTHS, SEASONS

Sunday	domenica	*domeneeka*
Monday	lunedì	*loonedee*
Tuesday	martedì	*martedee*
Wednesday	mercoledì	*mairkoledee*
Thursday	giovedì	*jovedee*
Friday	venerdì	*venairdee*
Saturday	sabato	*sabato*
January	gennaio	*jen-na-yo*
February	febbraio	*feb-bra-yo*
March	marzo	*martzo*
April	aprile	*apreelay*
May	maggio	*maj-jo*
June	giugno	*joon-yo*
July	luglio	*lool-yo*
August	agosto	*agosto*
September	settembre	*set-tembray*
October	ottobre	*ot-tobray*
November	novembre	*novembray*
December	dicembre	*deechembray*
Spring	primavera	*preemavaira*
Summer	estate	*estatay*
Autumn	autunno	*owtoon-no*
Winter	inverno	*eenvairno*
Christmas	Natale	*natalay*
Christmas Eve	la Vigilia di Natale	*veejeel-ya dee natalay*
Good Friday	Venerdì Santo	*venairdee santo*
Easter	Pasqua	*paskwa*
New Year	Capodanno	*kapodan-no*
New Year's Eve	San Silvestro	*san seelvestro*
Whitsun	Pentecoste	*pentaykostay*

NUMBERS

0 zero *tzairo*
1 uno *oono*
2 due *doo-ay*
3 tre *tray*
4 quattro *kwat-tro*
5 cinque *cheenkway*
6 sei *say*
7 sette *set-tay*
8 otto *ot-to*
9 nove *no-vay*

10 dieci *dee-aychee*
11 undici *oon-deechee*
12 dodici *doh-deechee*
13 tredici *tray-deechee*
14 quattordici *kwat-tor-deechee*
15 quindici *kween-deechee*
16 sedici *say-deechee*
17 diciassette *deechas-set-tay*
18 diciotto *deechot-to*
19 diciannove *deechan-no-vay*

20 venti *ventee*
21 ventuno *vent-oono*
22 ventidue *ventee-doo-ay*
30 trenta *trenta*
31 trentuno *trentoono*
32 trentadue *trentadoo-ay*
40 quaranta *kwaranta*
50 cinquanta *cheenkwanta*
60 sessanta *ses-santa*
70 settanta *set-tanta*
80 ottanta *ot-tanta*
90 novanta *novanta*
100 cento *chento*
110 centodieci *chento-dee-aychee*
200 duecento *doo-ay-chento*
1,000 mille *meelay*
10,000 diecimila *dee-aycheemeela*
20,000 ventimila *venteemeela*
50,000 cinquantamila *cheenkwantameela*
54,250 cinquantaquattromila duecentocinquanta *cheenkwanta-kwat-tro-meela doo-ay-chento-cheenkwanta*
100,000 centomila *chentomeela*
1,000,000 un milione *oon meel-yonay*

Note that thousands are written 1.000, 10.000 etc in Italian.

TIME

today	oggi	oj-jee
yesterday	ieri	yairee
tomorrow	domani	domanee
the day before yesterday	l'altro ieri	laltro yairee
the day after tomorrow	dopodomani	dopodomanee
this week	questa settimana	kwesta set-teemana
last week	la settimana scorsa	set-teemana skorsa
next week	la settimana prossima	set-teemana pros-seema
this morning	stamattina	stamat-teena
this afternoon	questo pomeriggio	kwesto pomereej-jo
this evening	stasera	stasaira
tonight	stanotte	stanot-tay
yesterday afternoon	ieri pomeriggio	yairee pomereej-jo
last night	ieri sera, ieri notte	yairee saira, yairee not-tay
tomorrow morning	domani mattina	domanee mat-teena
tomorrow night	domani sera	domanee saira
in three days	tra tre giorni	tra tray jornee
three days ago	tre giorni fa	tray jornee fa
late	tardi	tardee
early	presto	presto
soon	presto	presto
later on	più tardi	p-yoo tardee
at the moment	in questo momento	een kwesto momento
second	un secondo	sekondo
minute	un minuto	meenooto
two minutes	due minuti	doo-ay meenootee
quarter of an hour	un quarto d'ora	kwarto dora
half an hour	mezz'ora	medzora

20

three quarters of an hour	tre quarti d'ora	*tray kwartee dora*
hour	un'ora	*ora*
day	un giorno	*jorno*
week	una settimana	*set-teemana*
fortnight, two weeks	quindici giorni	*kween-deechee jornee*
month	un mese	*mayzay*
year	un anno	*an-no*
that day	quel giorno	*kwel jorno*
every day	ogni giorno	*on-yee jorno*
all day	tutto il giorno	*toot-to eel jorno*
the next day	il giorno dopo	*jorno dopo*

TELLING THE TIME

The hour is expressed in Italian by the ordinal number only: **sono le due** 'it's two o'clock'; 'at two o'clock' **alle due**. There is no equivalent of 'o'clock'. To say 'half past', add **e mezza** after the hour: **sono le due e mezza** 'it's half past two'. To say 'quarter past', add **e un quarto** 'and a quarter' to the hour: **sono le tre e un quarto** is 'it's a quarter past three'.

Quarter to the hour is expressed either by adding **e tre quarti** 'and three quarters' to the hour, or adding **meno un quarto** 'less a quarter' to the next hour. 'It's a quarter to eight' is therefore **sono le sette e tre quarti** OR **sono le otto meno un quarto**.

To express minutes past the hour, add the minutes to the hour: 'it's seven forty' **sono le sette e quaranta**. Minutes to the hour are expressed by adding **meno** followed by the number of minutes to the next hour: 'it's twenty to eight' **sono le otto meno venti**.

There are no equivalents of am and pm in Italian, although you could use **di mattina/del mattino** 'in the morning', **di/del pomeriggio** 'in the afternoon', **di sera** 'in the evening' and **di notte** 'at night'. For example: '10 am' **le dieci di mattina/del mattino**; '6 pm' **le sei di/del pomeriggio**; '10 pm' **le dieci di sera**; '2 am' **le due di notte** (but also **le due del mattino**)

The 24-hour clock is used much more frequently than in the

UK, both in the written form as in timetables, and verbally as in enquiry offices and when making appointments.

what time is it?	che ore sono?	*kay oray sono?*
it's one o'clock	è l'una	*eh loona*
it's two/three/four o'clock	sono le due/tre/quattro	*sono lay doo-ay/tray/kwat-tro*
ten past one	l'una e dieci	*loona ay dee-aychee*
quarter past one	l'una e un quarto	*loona ay oon kwarto*
half past one	l'una e mezza	*loona ay medza*
twenty to two	le due meno venti	*lay doo-ay mayno ventee*
quarter to two	le due meno un quarto	*lay doo-ay mayno oon kwarto*
two o'clock	le due	*lay doo-ay*
13.00	le tredici	*lay tray-deechee*
16.30	le sedici e trenta	*lay say-deechee ay trenta*
at half past five	alle cinque e mezza	*al-lay cheenkway ay medza*
at seven o'clock	alle sette	*al-lay set-tay*
noon	mezzogiorno	*medzojorno*
midnight	mezzanotte	*medzanot-tay*

THE CALENDAR

The cardinal numbers on page 19 are used to express the date in Italian, except for the first when the ordinal **il primo** is used:

the first of May	il primo maggio	*eel preemo maj-jo*
the second of September	il due settembre	*eel doo-ay set-tembray*
the twentieth of June	il venti giugno	*eel ventee joon-yo*

HOTELS

Hotels in Italy are classified according to the familiar star system: one, two, three, four and five stars. At the bottom of the range you'll find **locande** (one-star hotels) and **pensioni** (one- or two-star hotels). The prices are displayed in the rooms and they do not always include breakfast, but should include service charges and taxes.

In some areas, the local **APT** (**Azienda di Promozione Turistica**) can supply information about hotels, but in others tourism is co-ordinated by an **AAST** (**Azienda Autonoma di Soggiorno e Turismo**). It is also possible to obtain a list of hotels from information offices in stations and airports. If you arrive in a town without having booked beforehand, go directly to the **APT** or to the **AAST** for help. Leaflets will be available in English and usually at least one person there will speak English.

Hotel breakfasts usually consist of a **brioche** (a type of croissant) or bread, butter and jam, and coffee or tea. Some hotels may provide an English breakfast on request.

USEFUL WORDS AND PHRASES

balcony	il balcone	*bal-konay*
bath *(tub)*	la vasca da bagno	*vaska da ban-yo*
bathroom	il bagno	*ban-yo*
bed	il letto	*let-to*
bed and breakfast	camera con colazione	*kamaira kon kolatz-yonay*
bed and breakfast hotel	la pensione familiare	*penz-yonay fameel-yaray*
bedroom	la camera da letto	*kamaira da let-to*
bill	il conto	*konto*
breakfast	la prima colazione	*preema kolatz-yonay*
car park	il parcheggio	*parkej-jo*
dining room	la sala da pranzo	*sala da prantzo*

dinner	la cena	*chayna*
double bed	il letto matrimoniale	*let-to matreemon-yalay*
double room	la stanza doppia	*stantza doppee-a*
foyer	la hall	*oll*
full board	la pensione completa	*pens-yonay komplayta*
guesthouse	la pensione,	*pens-yonay*
	la locanda	*lokanda*
half board	la mezza pensione	*medza pens-yonay*
hotel	l'albergo, l'hotel	*albairgo, oh-tel*
key	la chiave	*k-yavay*
lift	l'ascensore	*ashen-soray*
lounge	il salone	*salonay*
lunch	il pranzo,	*prantzo*
	la seconda colazione	*sekonda kolatz-yonay*
maid	la cameriera	*kamair-yaira*
manager	il direttore	*deeret-toray*
receipt	la ricevuta	*reechevoota*
reception	la reception	*'reception'*
receptionist	il/la receptionist	*'receptionist'*
restaurant	il ristorante	*reestorantay*
room	la camera, la stanza	*kamaira, stantza*
room service	il servizio in camera	*serveetz-yo een kamaira*
shower	la doccia	*docha*
single bed	il letto singolo	*let-to seengolo*
single room	la stanza singola	*stantza seengola*
toilet	la toilette	*twalet*
twin room	la stanza con due letti	*stantza kon doo-ay lettee*
washbasin	il lavabo	*lavabo*

Have you any vacancies?
Avete una stanza libera?
avaytay oona stantza leebaira

I have a reservation
Ho prenotato una stanza
oh praynotato oona stantza

I'd like a single room
Vorrei una stanza singola
vor-ray oona stantza seengola

I'd like a room with a bathroom/balcony
Vorrei una stanza con bagno/con il balcone
vor-ray oona stantza kon ban-yo/kon eel bal-konay

I'd like a room for one night/three nights
Vorrei una stanza per una notte/tre notti
vor-ray oona stantza pair oona not-tay/tray not-tee

What is the charge per night?
Quanto si paga per notte?
kwanto see paga pair not-tay

I don't know yet how long I'll stay
Non so ancora quanto tempo rimarrò
non so ankora kwanto tempo reemarro

When is breakfast/dinner?
A che ora viene servita la colazione/la cena?
a kay ora v-yaynay serveeta la kolatz-yonay/la chayna

Please wake me at 7 o'clock
Mi svegli, per favore, alle sette
mee zvel-yee pair favoray al-lay set-tay

Can I have breakfast in my room?
Potrei avere la colazione in camera?
potray avairay la kolatz-yonay een kamaira

I'd like to have some laundry done
Vorrei far pulire alcuni indumenti
vor-ray far pooleeray alkoonee eendoomentee

25

I'll be back at 10 o'clock
Tornerò alle dieci
tornairo al-lay dee-aychee

My room number is 205
Il mio numero di stanza è duecentocinque
eel mee-o noomero dee stantza eh doo-aychentocheenkway

My booking was for a double room
Avevo prenotato una stanza doppia
avayvo praynotato oona stantza dop-pia

I asked for a room with an en-suite bathroom
Avevo chiesto una stanza con bagno
avayvo k-yaysto oona stantza kon ban-yo

There is no toilet paper in the bathroom
Non c'è carta igienica in bagno
non cheh karta eej-yeneeka een ban-yo

The window won't open
La finestra non si apre
la feenestra non see apray

The lift/shower isn't working
L'ascensore/la doccia non funziona
lashen-soray/la docha non foontz-yona

There isn't any hot water
Non c'è acqua calda
non cheh akwa kalda

The socket in the bathroom doesn't work
La presa di corrente del bagno non funziona
la prayza dee kor-rentay del ban-yo non foontz-yona

I'm leaving tomorrow
Parto domani
parto domanee

When do I have to vacate the room?
Entro che ora devo liberare la camera?
entro kay ora dayvo leebairaray la kamaira

Can I have the bill please?
Mi da il conto per favore?
mee da eel konto pair favoray

I'll pay by credit card
Pago con la carta di credito
pago kon la karta dee kraydeeto

I'll pay cash
Pago in contanti
pago een kontantee

Can you get me a taxi?
Potrebbe chiamarmi un taxi per favore?
potrayb-bay k-yamarmee oon 'taxi' pair favoray

Can you recommend another hotel?
Potrebbe consigliarmi un altro albergo?
potrayb-bay konseel-yarmee oon altro albairgo

THINGS YOU'LL SEE

albergo	hotel
ascensore	lift
bagno	bathroom
camera con prima colazione	bed and breakfast
camera doppia	double room
camera singola	single room
cena	dinner
colazione	breakfast
completo	no vacancies
conto	bill
doccia	shower

→

entrata	entrance/way in
locanda	guesthouse
mezza pensione	half board
parcheggio	car park
parcheggio riservato agli ospiti dell'albergo	parking reserved for hotel patrons only
pensione	guesthouse
pensione completa	full board
pianterreno	ground floor
pranzo	lunch
prenotazione	reservation
primo piano	first floor
scale	stairs
seconda colazione	lunch
spingere	push
stanza con due letti	twin room
tirare	pull
uscita d'emergenza	emergency exit

REPLIES YOU MAY BE GIVEN

Mi spiace, siamo al completo
I'm sorry, we're full

Non ci sono più camere singole/doppie
There are no single/double rooms left

Per quante notti?
For how many nights?

Come vuole pagare?
How will you be paying?

Pagamento anticipato, per favore
Please pay in advance

Dovete liberare la stanza entro mezzogiorno
You must vacate the room by midday

CAMPING AND CARAVANNING

Campsites in Italy usually have excellent facilities. Prices differ according to the size of tent (**casetta** = 'little house'; **canadese** = 'two man tent'), and/or the number of people sharing it. You can generally pay for a parking space next to the tent. Moving the car at certain times, for example mealtimes, is forbidden as it raises dust. If you go out in the evening you will not be allowed to bring your car back inside the site after midnight, but there are often parking facilities just outside.

Most campsites have electricity generators, for the use of which a small daily fee will be added to your bill. Toilet and washing facilities are generally very good. You may have to pay for a hot shower with coins or tokens – which you insert into a machine attached to the shower. If tokens (**gettoni**) are needed these will be available at the campsite office. Cold showers are free. The campsite office usually acts as a mini-bank as well. You can deposit all your money there and withdraw it on a daily basis. The office will also exchange foreign currency.

USEFUL WORDS AND PHRASES

bonfire	il falò	*falo*
bucket	il secchio	*sek-yo*
go camping	andare in campeggio	*andaray een kampej-jo*
campsite	il campeggio	*kampej-jo*
caravan	la roulotte	*roolot*
caravan site	il campeggio	*kampej-jo*
cooking utensils	gli utensili da cucina	*ootenseelee da koocheena*
drinking water	l'acqua potabile	*akwa pota-beelay*
ground sheet	il telone impermeabile	*telonay eempair-may-abeelay*
hitchhike	fare l'autostop	*faray lowto-stop*
rope	la fune, la corda	*foonay, korda*

29

rubbish	l'immondizia	*eem-mondeetzee-a*
rucksack	lo zaino	*tza-eeno*
saucepans	le pentole	*pentolay*
sleeping bag	il sacco a pelo	*sak-ko a paylo*
tent	la tenda	*tenda*
tokens	i gettoni	*jet-tonee*
youth hostel	l'ostello della gioventù	*ostel-lo del-la joventoo*

Can I camp here?
Posso campeggiare qui?
pos-so kampej-jaray kwee

Can we park the caravan here?
Possiamo parcheggiare la roulotte qui?
poss-yamo parkej-jaray la roolot kwee

Where is the nearest campsite/caravan site?
Qual è il campeggio più vicino?
kwal eh eel kampej-jo p-yoo veecheeno

What is the charge per night?
Quanto si paga per notte?
kwanto see paga pair not-tay

I only want to stay for one night
Vorrei fermarmi solo una notte
vor-ray fairmarmee solo oona not-tay

How much is it for a week?
Quanto mi viene a costare per una settimana?
kwanto mee v-yaynay a kostaray pair oona set-teemana

We're leaving tomorrow
Partiamo domani
part-yamo domanee

Where is the kitchen?
Dov'è la cucina?
doveh la koocheena

Can I light a fire here?
Posso accendere il fuoco qui?
pos-so achendairay eel fwoko kwee

Can I have some tokens for the shower?
Potrei avere alcuni gettoni per la doccia?
potray avairay alkoonee jet-tonee pair la docha

Where can I get ...?
Dove posso trovare...?
dovay pos-so trovaray

Is there any drinking water?
C'è acqua potabile?
cheh akwa pota-beelay

THINGS YOU'LL SEE

acqua potabile	drinking water
a persona	per person
campeggio	campsite
cucina	kitchen
docce	showers
gabinetti	toilets
ostello della gioventù	youth hostel
rimorchio	trailer
roulotte	caravan, trailer
tariffa	charge
tenda	tent
vietato accendere fuochi	no campfires
vietato campeggiare	no camping

VILLAS AND APARTMENTS

In Italy you can arrange to rent a flat in travel agencies or from an estate agent. If you make a reservation, you will be asked to pay a deposit in advance.

When you arrive in the tourist resort where you reserved the villa or apartment, you will have to sign a contract. Your name, the date of rental, the address of the apartment, deposits, etc will be specified in this contract. You may be asked to pay for certain 'extras' not included in the original price (in particular tourist taxes). Gas and electricity are normally included, while cleaning seldom is. It's a good idea to ask about an inventory at the start, rather than be told something is missing later just as you are about to leave; sometimes you will find an inventory in the apartment (in a drawer or in a cupboard). Usually, you are not required to sign it.

You may be asked for a deposit, in case you break something. Make sure this is specified in the contract you signed. You will get your money back when you leave.

USEFUL WORDS AND PHRASES

bath *(tub)*	la vasca da bagno	v*a*ska da b*a*n-yo
bathroom	il bagno	b*a*n-yo
bedroom	la camera da letto	k*a*maira da l*e*t-to
blocked	intasato	eentaz*a*to
boiler	lo scaldabagno	skaldab*a*n-yo
broken	rotto	r*o*t-to
caretaker	il portinaio	porteen*i*-o
(female)	la portinaia	porteen*i*-a
central heating	il riscaldamento centrale	reeskaldam*e*nto chentr*a*lay
cleaner	l'uomo delle pulizie	w*o*mo d*e*l-lay pooleetz*ee*-ay
(female)	la donna delle pulizie	d*o*n-na d*e*l-lay pooleetz*ee*-ay

32

cooker	il fornello	*fornel-lo*
deposit *(security)*	la cauzione	*kowtz-yonay*
(part payment)	la caparra	*kapar-ra*
drain	lo scarico	*skareeko*
dustbin	il bidone della spazzatura	*beedonay del-la spatz-zatoora*
duvet	il piumino	*p-yoomeeno*
electrician	l'elettricista	*elet-treecheesta*
electricity	l'elettricità	*elet-treecheeta*
estate agent	l'agente immobiliare	*ajentay eem-mobeelyaray*
fridge	il frigorifero	*freegoreefairo*
fusebox	la scatola dei fusibili	*skatola day foozeebeelee*
gas	il gas	*'gas'*
grill	la griglia	*greel-ya*
heater	il calorifero	*kaloreefairo*
iron	il ferro da stiro	*fair-ro da steero*
ironing board	la tavola da stiro	*tavola da steero*
keys	le chiavi	*k-ya-vee*
kitchen	la cucina	*koocheena*
leak *(noun)*	la perdita	*pairdeeta*
(verb)	perdere	*pairdairay*
light	la luce	*loochay*
living room	il soggiorno	*soj-jorno*
maid	la cameriera	*kamair-yaira*
pillow	il cuscino	*koosheeno*
pillow slip	la federa	*fedaira*
plumber	l'idraulico	*eedrowleeko*
refund	il rimborso	*reemborso*
sheets	le lenzuola	*lentzwola*
shower	la doccia	*docha*
sink	il lavandino	*lavandeeno*
stopcock	il rubinetto d'arresto	*roobeenet-to dar-resto*
swimming pool	la piscina	*peesheena*
tap	il rubinetto	*roobeenet-to*
toilet	il gabinetto	*gabeenet-to*

towel	l'asciugamano	*ashoogam<u>a</u>no*
washing machine	la lavatrice	*lavatr<u>ee</u>chay*
water	l'acqua	*<u>a</u>kwa*
water heater	lo scaldaacqua	*skalda-<u>a</u>kwa*

I'd like to rent an apartment/villa for ... days
Vorrei affittare un appartamento/una villa per... giorni
vor-r<u>ay</u> af-feet-t<u>a</u>ray oon ap-partam<u>e</u>nto/<u>oo</u>na v<u>ee</u>l-la pair ... j<u>o</u>rnee

Do I have to pay a deposit?
Devo versare una cauzione?
d<u>a</u>yvo vairs<u>a</u>ray <u>oo</u>na kowtz-y<u>o</u>nay

Does the price include gas and electricity?
Il gas e l'elettricità sono inclusi nel prezzo?
eel 'gas' ay lelet-treecheet<u>a</u> s<u>o</u>no eenkl<u>oo</u>zee nel pr<u>e</u>tzo

Where is this item?
Dove si trova questo oggetto?
d<u>o</u>vay see tr<u>o</u>va kw<u>e</u>sto oj-j<u>e</u>t-to

Please take it off the inventory
Lo tolga dall'inventario, per favore
lo t<u>o</u>lga dal-leenventar-yo pair fav<u>o</u>ray

We've broken this
Abbiamo rotto questo
abb-y<u>a</u>mo r<u>o</u>t-to kw<u>e</u>sto

This was broken when we arrived
Era già rotto quando siamo arrivati
<u>a</u>yra j<u>a</u> r<u>o</u>t-to kw<u>a</u>ndo s-y<u>a</u>mo ar-reev<u>a</u>tee

This was missing when we arrived
Non c'era quando siamo arrivati
non ch<u>a</u>yra kw<u>a</u>ndo s-y<u>a</u>mo ar-reev<u>a</u>tee

Can I have my deposit back?
Potrei riavere la cauzione?
potray ree-avairay la kowtz-yonay

Can we have an extra bed?
Potremmo avere un letto in più?
potraym-mo avairay oon let-to een p-yoo

Can we have more crockery/cutlery?
Potremmo avere ancora un po' di stoviglie/posate?
potraym-mo avairay ankora oon po dee stoveel-yay/pozatay

When does the maid come?
Quando viene la cameriera?
kwando v-yaynay la kamair-yaira

Where can I buy/find ...?
Dove posso comprare/trovare...?
dovay pos-so kompraray/trovaray

How does the water heater work?
Come funziona lo scaldaacqua?
komay foontz-yona lo skalda-akwa

Do you do ironing/baby-sitting?
Sà stirare/badare ai bambini?
sa steeraray/badaray i bambeenee

Do you prepare lunch/dinner?
È in grado di preparare il pranzo/la cena?
eh een grado dee praypararay eel prantzo/la chayna

Do we have to pay extra or is it included?
Dobbiamo pagarlo a parte o è incluso nel prezzo?
dobb-yamo pagarlo a partay oh eh eenkloozo nel pret-zo

The shower doesn't work
La doccia non funziona
la docha non foontz-yona

The sink is blocked
Il lavandino è intasato
eel lavandeeno eh eentazato

The sink/toilet is leaking
Il lavandino/gabinetto perde
eel lavandeeno/gabeenet-to pairday

There's a burst pipe
Si è rotto un tubo
see eh rot-to oon toobo

The rubbish has not been collected for a week
Non portano via la spazzatura da una settimana
non portano vee-a la spatz-zatoora da oona set-teemana

There's no electricity/gas/water
Non c'è elettricità/gas/acqua
non cheh elet-treecheeta/'gas'/akwa

Can you mend it today?
Può ripararlo oggi?
pwo reepararlo oj-jee

Send your bill to ...
Mandi il conto a...
mandee eel konto a

I'm staying at ...
Sto a...
sto a

Thank you for everything!
Grazie di tutto!
gratzee-ay dee toot-to

See you again next year!
Al prossimo anno!
al pros-seemo an-no

MOTORING

In Italy you drive on the right and overtake on the left. On dual carriageways you may stay in the left-hand lane if heavy traffic has taken over the right-hand lane. Normally you may move from the right to the left-hand lane only for turning or overtaking. On three-lane roads with traffic flowing in both directions the central lane is for overtaking only.

At junctions where there are no indications or traffic lights, you must give way to traffic coming from the right, except in the case of a service station exit, a private road or a track entering the main road. Usually, a diamond-shaped yellow sign tells you that you have right of way; the end of this right of way is indicated by a similar sign with a bar through it. An upside-down red triangle or a 'STOP' sign indicates that you must give way to all vehicles coming both from the right and from the left.

In built-up areas the speed limit is 50km/h (31 mph). On open roads (if not otherwise indicated) it is 90km/h (56 mph) and on motorways it is 130 km/h (81 mph).

If you break down and are forced to stop in the middle of the road, you must place a red triangle 50 metres behind your vehicle to warn other drivers. All drivers must carry this triangle – which can be rented from the offices of the **ACI (Automobile Club Italiano)** on entering Italy and then returned on leaving the country.

There are emergency telephones on most motorways. If you break down on the **Autostrada del Sole** (Milan-Rome) or on another main motorway there are emergency telephones on the right side of the motorway at intervals of 1 or 2 kms. Generally, it is illegal to walk along the motorway or hitchhike, but if the breakdown occurs between two telephones, you are allowed to walk to the next emergency telephone. (See also EMERGENCIES page 107.)

Most town centres are pedestrian precincts, and if you park where you are not supposed to, your car will be towed away. You should park either in a free parking area or in a paying car park or garage. Charges are displayed on a notice board in the car park. You'll be given a parking ticket when you arrive, or, if there is a car-park attendant, he will place a ticket on your windscreen and you pay on departure.

SOME COMMON ROAD SIGNS

accendere i fari	headlights on
attenzione	watch out, caution
autostrada	motorway (with toll)
banchina non transitabile	soft verge
caduta massi	falling rocks
centro	town centre
code	traffic queues ahead
controllo automatico della velocità	automatic speed monitor
cunetta o dosso	ditch
deviazione	diversion
disporsi su due file	two-lane traffic
divieto di accesso	no entry
divieto di fermata	no stopping
divieto di transito	no thoroughfare
dogana	customs
escluso frontisti	residents only
fine del tratto autostradale	end of motorway
ghiaccio	ice
incrocio	junction
incrocio pericoloso	dangerous junction/crossroads
informazioni turistiche	tourist information
lavori in corso	roadworks
nebbia	fog
non oltrepassare	no trespassing
pagare qui	pay here
parcheggio a giorni alterni	parking on alternate days
parcheggio a pagamento	paying car-park

→

---

parcheggio custodito	car park with attendant
parcheggio incustodito	unattended car park
pedaggio	toll
pedoni	pedestrians
pericolo	danger
pista ciclabile	cycle track
provinciale	main road
rallentare	reduce speed
scuola	school
senso unico	one way
sosta vietata	no parking
sottopassaggio	subway
strada a fondo cieco	blind alley
strada camionabile	route for heavy vehicles
strada ghiacciata	ice on road
strada provinciale	main road
strada sdrucciolevole	slippery road
strada secondaria	secondary road
strada statale	main road
superstrada	motorway
uscita camion	works exit
veicoli lenti	crawler lane
zona a traffico limitato	restricted traffic area
zona pedonale	pedestrian precinct

USEFUL WORDS AND PHRASES

automatic	con il cambio automatico	*kon eel kam-bee-o owtomateeko*
bonnet	il cofano	*kofano*
boot	il portabagagli	*portabagal-yee*
brake	il freno	*frayno*
breakdown	il guasto	*gwasto*
car	l'automobile, la macchina	*owtomobeelay, mak-keena*

caravan	la roulotte	*roolot*
car ferry	il traghetto	*traget-to*
car park	il parcheggio	*parkej-jo*
clutch	la frizione	*freetz-yonay*
crossroads	l'incrocio	*eenkrocho*
drive	guidare	*gweedaray*
engine	il motore	*motoray*
exhaust	lo scappamento	*skap-pamento*
fanbelt	la cinghia della ventola	*cheeng-ya del-la ventola*
garage *(repairs)*	l'autorimessa	*owtoreemes-sa*
(for petrol)	la stazione di servizio	*statz-yonay dee sairveetz-yo*
gear	il cambio	*kam-bee-o*
gear box	la scatola del cambio	*skatola del kam-bee-o*
gears	le marce	*marchay*
headlights	i fari	*faree*
indicator	l'indicatore di direzione, la freccia	*eendeekatoray dee deeretz-yonay, frech-cha*
junction	l'incrocio	*eenkrocho*
(motorway entry)	raccordo di entrata	*rak-kordo dee entrata*
(motorway exit)	raccordo di uscita	*rak-kordo dee oosheeta*
licence	la patente	*patentay*
lorry	il camion, l'autocarro	*kam-yon, owtokar-ro*
manual	con il cambio manuale	*kon eel kam-bee-o manwalay*
mirror	lo specchietto	*spekk-yet-to*
motorbike	la motocicletta	*motocheeklet-ta*
motorway	l'autostrada	*owtostrada*
number plate	la targa	*targa*
petrol	la benzina	*bendzeena*
petrol station	la stazione di servizio	*statz-yonay dee sairveetz-yo*
rear lights	i fari posteriori	*faree postair-yoree*
road	la strada	*strada*

spares	i pezzi di ricambio	*petzee dee reekam-bee-o*
spark plug	la candela	*kandayla*
speed	la velocità	*velocheeta*
speed limit	il limite di velocità	*leemeetay dee velocheeta*
speedometer	il tachimetro	*takeemetro*
steering wheel	il volante	*volantay*
traffic lights	il semaforo	*semaforo*
trailer	il rimorchio	*reemork-yo*
tyre	la gomma	*gom-ma*
van	il furgone	*foorgonay*
warning triangle	il triangolo	*tree-angolo*
wheel	la ruota	*rwota*
windscreen	il parabrezza	*parabretza*
windscreen wiper	il tergicristallo	*tairjee-kreestal-lo*

Could you check the oil/water level, please?
Potrebbe controllare il livello dell'olio/dell'acqua, per favore?
potrayb-bay kontrol-laray eel leevel-lo del ol-yo/del akwa pair favoray

Fill her up please!
Faccia il pieno, per cortesia!
facha eel p-yayno pair kortayzee-a

I'd like 35 litres of 4-star
Mi dia trentacinque litri di super, per favore
mee dee-a trentacheenkway leetree dee soopair pair favoray

Do you do repairs?
Effettua riparazioni?
ef-fet-too-a reeparatz-yonee

Can you repair the clutch?
Può ripararmi la frizione?
pwo reepararmee la freetz-yonay

There is something wrong with the engine
C'è qualcosa che non va nel motore
cheh kwalkoza kay non va nel motoray

The engine is overheating
Il motore si surriscalda
eel motoray see soor-reeskalda

I need a new tyre
Ho bisogno di una gomma nuova
oh beezon-yo dee oona gom-ma nwova

Can you replace this?
Può sostituirlo?
pwo sosteetoo-eerlo

The indicator is not working
La freccia non funziona
la frech-cha non foontz-yona

How long will it take?
Quanto tempo ci vorrà?
kwanto tempo chee vor-ra

Where can I park?
Dove posso parcheggiare?
dovay pos-so parkej-jaray

I'd like to hire a car
Vorrei noleggiare una macchina
vor-ray nolej-jaray oona mak-keena

I'd like an automatic/a manual
Vorrei una macchina con il cambio automatico/manuale
*vor-ray oona mak-keena kon eel kam-bee-o owtomateeko/
    manwalay*

How much is it for one day?
Quanto costa per un giorno?
kwanto kosta pair oon jorno

Is there a mileage charge?
C'è un supplemento per il chilometraggio?
cheh oon soop-plemento pair eel keelometraj-jo

When do I have to return it?
Quando devo riportarla?
kwando dayvo reeportarla

Where is the nearest petrol station?
Dov'è la stazione di servizio più vicina?
doveh la statz-yonay dee sairveetz-yo p-yoo veecheena

How do I get to ...?
Può dirmi come andare a...?
pwo deermee komay andaray a

Is this the road to ...?
È questa la strada per...?
eh kwesta la strada pair

Which is the quickest way to ...?
Qual è la strada più breve per...?
kwal eh la strada p-yoo brayvay pair

DIRECTIONS YOU MAY BE GIVEN

a destra	right
a sinistra	left
dritto	straight on
giri a destra	turn right
giri a sinistra	turn left
il primo/la prima a destra	first on the right
il secondo/la seconda a sinistra	second on the left
vada oltre...	go past the ...

THINGS YOU'LL SEE

acqua	water
area di servizio	service area

$\longrightarrow$

43

aspirapolvere	vacuum cleaner
autolavaggio	car wash
autorimessa	garage (for repairs)
benzina	petrol
benzina normale	two- or three-star petrol
benzina senza piombo	unleaded petrol
benzina super	four-star petrol
casello autostradale	motorway toll booth
cera per auto	car wax
code	traffic queue
deviazione	diversion
gasolio	diesel oil
gommista	tyre repairs
guidare a passo d'uomo	drive at walking speed
liquido tergicristallo	screen wash
olio	oil
raccordo autostradale	motorway junction
spegnere il motore	switch off engine
spingere	push
stazione di servizio	service station
uscita	exit
tirare	pull
vietato fumare	no smoking

THINGS YOU'LL HEAR

Vuole una macchina con il cambio automatico o manuale?
Would you like an automatic or a manual?

Esibisca la patente, per favore
May I see your licence, please?

Mi fa vedere il passaporto, per favore?
May I see your passport, please?

TRAVELLING AROUND

RAIL TRAVEL

Rail travel is so cheap in Italy that it is very widely used. During the tourist season travelling by train can be difficult so, wherever possible, you should book your seat well in advance. Children under four years of age not occupying a seat travel free, and there is a half-price fare for children aged between four and twelve years. Considerable reductions are available for families and individuals on short-term season tickets. Couchettes are available on most domestic long-distance night services and most long-distance trains have restaurant cars. On shorter journeys there will be a trolley on the train from which you can buy sandwiches and soft drinks. In main stations, platform vendors pass by the train windows.

Trains on Italian State Railways (**Ferrovie dello Stato** or **FS**) are classified as follows:

EC (**Eurocity**): very fast international train, with first and second class compartments. A supplement must be paid in advance but there is no charge for booking a seat in advance.

IC (**Intercity**): very fast national train. Most **IC**s have first and second class, but there are still a few of them with first class only. It's best to check this before departure. A supplement must be paid in advance but reserving a seat is free.

Espresso: long-distance fast train. No supplement required.

Diretto: long-distance train stopping at main stations.

Regionale: small local train stopping at nearly every station.

You should find out in advance whether you will be taking an **IC** or **EC** train and ask to pay the supplement when you buy your ticket. If you have a return ticket, you should validate the return journey by stamping the date on it on the day you return. In most stations, there are ticket-stamping machines but, in small stations, you should go to the ticket office.

LONG-DISTANCE BUS TRAVEL

People rarely travel long distances by coach in Italy as the rail service is so cheap and travelling by train is quicker. Local coaches for small towns and places of interest are generally inexpensive and the service frequent. The coaches often have a system similar to that of local buses: when you enter you stamp your ticket in the ticket-stamping machine.

LOCAL PUBLIC TRANSPORT

In large cities there are several types of public transport: bus, trolley bus (**filobus**), tram and underground (**Metropolitana**). In some cities there is an integrated public transport system, which means that the same tickets can be used on all types of transport. Tickets are cheap and operate on a flat-fare basis. In most cities, they are valid for 60 to 75 minutes but in some they are only valid for a one-way trip. Tickets can be bought in the underground, at any newspaper kiosk, **tabaccaio** or ordinary bar with a '**vendita biglietti**' sign in the window. When you enter a bus, **filobus** etc, you must insert your ticket into a machine which stamps the time on it. The only restriction on use of the ticket is that you cannot re-enter the **Metropolitana** with the same ticket, even if you have not yet used up your 75 minutes. There are inspectors who make random checks, and if you are travelling without a valid ticket you can expect an on-the-spot fine of about 20,000 lire. In most places public transport is very quick and efficient. Smoking is forbidden on all local public transport.

TAXI AND BOAT

It is advisable not to travel in a taxi which does not have the 'taxi' sign on top. Taxis without this sign are private taxis and may charge astronomical prices. The marked taxis are reliable and efficient but they do have a high minimum charge. Moreover, there is always an extra charge for each item of luggage and for journeys undertaken at night.

In Venice (where of course there are no buses etc) you travel by **vaporetto**, a small passenger boat. You must buy your ticket in advance from the kiosk at **vaporetti** stops. There is a flat fare for all destinations. There are, however, special offers, such as cheap 24-hour tickets with which you can travel on any number of boats for any distance, starting from the time when you stamp your ticket at the boat stop (not from when you buy it).

USEFUL WORDS AND PHRASES

airport	l'aeroporto	*a-airoporto*
airport bus	l'autobus per	*owtoboos pair*
	l'aeroporto	*la-airoporto*
aisle seat	il posto vicino	*posto veecheeno*
	al corridoio	*al kor-reedo-yo*
adult	l'adulto	*adoolto*
baggage claim	il ritiro bagagli	*reeteero bagal-yee*
boarding card	la carta d'imbarco	*karta deembarko*
boat	la barca,	*barka,*
	il battello	*bat-taylo*
booking office	la biglietteria	*beel-yet-teree-a*
buffet	il buffet	*boofay*
bus	l'autobus	*owtoboos*
bus station	la stazione degli	*statz-yonay del-yee*
	autobus	*owtoboos*
bus stop	la fermata	*fermata del lowtoboos*
	dell'autobus	
check-in desk	l'accettazione	*achet-tatz-yonay*
	(bagagli)	*bagal-yee*
child	il bambino	*bambeeno*
(female)	la bambina	*bambeena*
coach *(bus)*	la corriera	*kor-ree-aira*
compartment	lo scompartimento	*skomparteemento*
connection	la coincidenza	*ko-eencheedentza*
couchette	la cuccetta	*kooch-chet-ta*
cruise	la crociera	*krochaira*
customs	la dogana	*dogana*

departure lounge	la sala d'attesa	*sala dat-tayza*
domestic	nazionale	*natz-yonalay*
emergency exit	l'uscita di sicurezza	*oosheeta dee seekooretza*
entrance	l'entrata	*entrata*
exit	l'uscita	*oosheeta*
fare	la tariffa	*tareef-fa*
ferry	il traghetto	*trag-et-to*
first class	la prima classe	*preema klas-say*
flight	il volo	*volo*
flight number	il numero del volo	*noomairo del volo*
gate	l'uscita	*oosheeta*
hand luggage	il bagaglio a mano	*bagal-yo a mano*
international	internazionale	*eentairnatz-yonalay*
left luggage office	il deposito bagagli	*depozeeto bagal-yee*
lost property office	l'ufficio oggetti smarriti	*oof-feecho ojet-tee zmar-reetee*
luggage trolley	il carrello	*kar-rel-lo*
network map	la piantina dei trasporti pubblici	*p-yanteena day tras-portee poob-bleechee*
non-smoking	non fumatori	*non foomatoree*
number 5 bus	l'autobus numero cinque	*owtoboos noomayro cheenkway*
passport	il passaporto	*pas-saporto*
platform	il binario	*beenaree-o*
railway	la ferrovia	*fer-rovee-a*
reserved seat	il posto riservato	*posto ree-sairvato*
restaurant car	il vagone ristorante	*vagonay reestorantay*
return ticket	il biglietto di andata e ritorno	*beel-yet-to dee andata ay reetorno*
seat	il posto	*posto*
second class	la seconda classe	*sekonda klas-say*
single ticket	la biglietto di sola andata	*beel-yet-to dee sola andata*
sleeper	il vagone letto	*vagonay let-to*
smoking	fumatori	*foomatoree*
station	la stazione	*statz-yonay*

subway	il sottopassaggio	*sot-topas-saj-jo*
taxi	il taxi	*'taxi'*
terminus	il capolinea	*kapoleenay-a*
ticket	il biglietto	*beel-yet-to*
timetable	l'orario	*orar-yo*
train	il treno	*trayno*
tram	il tram	*'tram'*
trolley bus	il filobus	*feeloboos*
underground	la metropolitana	*metro-poleetana*
waiting room	la sala d'attesa	*sala dat-tayza*
window seat	il posto vicino al finestrino	*posto veecheeno al feenestreeno*

AIR TRAVEL

I'd like a non-smoking seat please
Vorrei un posto per non fumatori, per favore
vor-ray oon posto pair non foomatoree pair favoray

I'd like a window seat please
Vorrei un posto vicino al finestrino
vor-ray oon posto veecheeno al feenestreeno

How long will the flight be delayed?
Con quanto ritardo partirà il volo?
kon kwanto reetardo parteera eel volo

Which gate for the flight to London?
Qual è l'uscita del volo per Londra?
kwal eh loosheeta del volo pair londra

RAIL AND BUS TRAVEL

When does the train/bus for Florence leave?
A che ora parte il treno/l'autobus per Firenze?
a kay ora partay eel trayno/lowtoboos pair feerentzay

49

When does the train/bus from Rome arrive?
A che ora arriva il treno/l'autobus da Roma?
a kay ora ar-reeva eel trayno/lowtoboos da roma

When is the next train/bus to Venice?
A che ora c'è il prossimo treno/autobus per Venezia?
a kay ora cheh eel pros-seemo trayno/owtoboos pair venetzee-a

When is the first/last train/bus to Turin?
A che ora c'è il primo/l'ultimo treno/autobus per Torino?
a kay ora cheh eel preemo/loolteemo trayno/owtoboos pair toreeno

What is the fare to Naples?
Quanto costa il biglietto per Napoli?
kwanto kosta eel beel-yet-to pair napolee

Do I have to change?
Devo cambiare?
dayvo kamb-yaray

Does the train/bus stop at Padua?
Il treno/l'autobus ferma a Padova?
eel trayno/lowtoboos fairma a padova

How long does it take to get to Trieste?
Quanto tempo ci s'impiega per andare a Trieste?
kwanto tempo chee seemp-yayga pair andaray a tree-estay

Where can I buy a ticket?
Dove posso comprare il biglietto?
dovay pos-so kompraray eel beel-yet-to

A single/return ticket to Bologna please
Un biglietto di sola andata/di andata e ritorno per Bologna, per favore
oon beel-yet-to dee sola andata/dee andata ay reetorno pair bolon-ya pair favoray

Could you help me get a ticket?
Potrebbe aiutarmi a prendere il biglietto?
potrayb-bay ı-ootarmee a prendairay eel beel-yet-to

Do I have to pay a supplement?
Devo pagare un supplemento?
dayvo pagaray oon soop-plemento

I'd like to reserve a seat
Vorrei prenotare un posto a sedere
vor-ray praynotaray oon posto a sedayray

REPLIES YOU MAY BE GIVEN

Il prossimo treno parte alle diciotto
The next train leaves at 18.00 hours

Deve cambiare a Firenze
Change at Florence

Deve pagare un supplemento
You must pay a supplement

Non ci sono più posti per Catania
There are no more seats available for Catania

Is this the right train/bus for Genoa?
È questo il treno/l'autobus per Genova?
eh kwesto eel trayno/lowtoboos pair jenova

Is this the right platform for the Palermo train?
È questo il binario del treno per Palermo?
eh kwesto eel beenaree-o del trayno pair palairmo

Which platform for the Perugia train?
A che binario parte il treno per Perugia?
a kay beenaree-o partay eel trayno pair perooja

Is the train/bus late?
Il treno/l'autobus è in ritardo?
eel trayno/lowtoboos eh een reetardo

Could you help me with my luggage please?
Potrebbe darmi una mano con i bagagli, per favore?
potrayb-bay darmee oona mano kon ee bagal-yee pair favoray

Is this a non-smoking compartment?
È uno scompartimento non fumatori?
eh oono skomparteemento non foomatoree

Is this seat free?
È libero questo posto?
eh leebairo kwesto posto

This seat is taken
Questo posto è occupato
kwesto posto eh ok-koopato

I have reserved this seat
Questo posto è riservato
kwesto posto eh ree-sairvato

May I open/close the window?
Posso aprire/chiudere il finestrino?
pos-so apreeray/k-yoodairay eel feenestreeno

When do we arrive in Bari?
A che ora arriviamo a Bari?
a kay ora arreev-yamo a baree

What station is this?
Che stazione è questa?
kay statz-yonay eh kwesta

Do we stop at Pisa?
Ci fermiamo a Pisa?
chee fairmee-amo a peeza

Would you keep an eye on my things for a moment?
Le dispiace dare un'occhiata alla mia roba per un momento?
lay deespee-achay daray oon okk-yata al-la mee-a roba pair oon momento

Is there a restaurant car on this train?
C'è un vagone ristorante su questo treno?
cheh oon vagonay reestorantay soo kwesto trayno

LOCAL PUBLIC TRANSPORT

Where is the nearest underground station?
Qual è la stazione della metropolitana più vicina?
kwal eh la statz-yonay del-la metro-poleetana p-yoo veecheena

Where is the bus station?
Dov'è la stazione degli autobus?
doveh la statz-yonay del-yee owtoboos

Which buses go to Mantua?
Quale autobus va a Mantova?
kwalay owtoboos va a mantova

How often do the buses to San Gimignano run?
Ogni quanto passa l'autobus per San Gimignano?
on-yee kwanto pas-sa lowtoboos pair san jeemeen-yano

Will you let me know when we're there?
Mi potrebbe avvertire quando arriviamo là?
mee potrayb-bay av-verteeray kwando ar-reev-yamo la

Do I have to get off yet?
Devo scendere qui?
dayvo shendairay kwee

How do you get to Asti?
Come posso andare ad Asti?
komay pos-so andaray ad astee

I want to go to Udine
Voglio andare a Udine
vol-yo andaray a oodeenay

Do you go near Enna?
Passa vicino ad Enna?
pas-sa veecheeno ad en-na

TAXI AND BOAT

To the airport please
All'aeroporto, per favore
alla-airoporto pair favoray

How much will it cost?
Quanto mi verrà a costare?
kwanto mee vair-ra a kostaray

Please stop here
Si fermi qui, per favore
see fairmee kwee pair favoray

Could you wait here for me and take me back?
Può aspettarmi qui per riportarmi indietro?
pwo aspet-tarmee kwee pair reeportarmee eend-yaytro

Where can I get the boat to Sirmione?
Dove posso prendere il battello per Sirmione?
dovay pos-so prendairay eel bat-tello pair seerm-yonay

THINGS YOU'LL SEE

abbonamento mensile	monthly ticket
abbonamento settimanale	weekly ticket
ai binari/treni	to the platforms/trains
arrivi	arrivals
bambini	children
biglietto	ticket
biglietto d'accesso ai treni	platform ticket
biglietto giornaliero	day ticket
biglietto valido per più corse	multi-journey ticket

→

cambiare	to change
cambio	bureau de change
capolinea	terminus
carrozza	carriage, car
controllo bagagli	baggage control
controllo biglietti	ticket inspection
controllo passaporti	passport control
cuccetta	sleeper
deposito bagagli	left luggage
diretto	long-distance train
discesa	exit
distributore automatico di biglietti	ticket machine
entrata	way in, entrance
è pericoloso sporgersi	it is dangerous to lean out
espresso	long-distance fast train
fermata	stop
Ferrovie dello Stato/FS	State Railways
fumatori	smokers
giro in barca	boat trip
informazioni	information
la domenica	Sundays
la domenica e i giorni festivi	Sundays and public holidays
libero	free
macchina obliteratrice	ticket-stamping machine
nazionale	domestic
non ferma a...	does not stop at ...
non fumatori	non-smokers
non parlare al conducente	do not speak to the driver
occupato	engaged, reserved
oggetti smarriti	lost property
ogni abuso sarà punito con...	penalty for misuse ...
ora locale	local time
orario	timetable
orario di volo	flight time
percorso	route

→

partenze	departures
passeggeri	passengers
porto	harbour, port
posti in piedi	standing room
posto (a sedere)	seat
posto prenotato	reserved seat
rapido	fast train
riservato ai non fumatori	non-smokers only
ritardo	delay
ritiro bagagli	baggage claim
sala d'attesa	waiting room
salita	entry
(segnale d')allarme	emergency alarm
solo il sabato/la domenica	Saturdays/Sundays only
spuntini, panini	snacks, sandwiches
supplemento rapido	supplement for fast train
tesserino	travel card
tragitto breve	short journey
uscita	exit
uscita di sicurezza	emergency exit
vagone	carriage, car
vagone letto	sleeper
vagone ristorante	restaurant car
viaggio	journey
vietato fumare	no smoking
vietato l'ingresso	no entry
vietato sporgersi	do not lean out
volo	flight
volo di linea	scheduled flight

THINGS YOU'LL HEAR

Ha bagagli?
Have you any luggage?

→

Fumatori o non fumatori?
Smoking or non-smoking?

Posto sul corridoio o vicino al finestrino?
Aisle seat or window seat?

Posso vedere il vostro passaporto/biglietto, per favore?
Can I see your passport/ticket, please?

I passeggeri in partenza per Roma sono pregati di recarsi all'imbarco
Passengers for Rome are requested to board

Recarsi all'uscita quattro, per favore
Please proceed to gate number four

Biglietti, prego
Tickets please

Il treno intercity numero 687 per Roma è in partenza dal binario tre
Intercity train number 687 for Rome is leaving from platform three

Il treno regionale numero 89 da Bologna è in arrivo al binario due
Local train number 89 from Bologna is approaching platform two

Il treno espresso numero 435 da Venezia viaggia con trenta minuti di ritardo
Express train number 435 from Venice is running thirty minutes late

Apra la valigia, per favore
Open your suitcase, please

RESTAURANTS

There are various types of places for eating out. For snacks the most common is the bar. These are open all day from early morning until about 10 pm. They are all licensed to sell alcohol and usually offer a variety of sandwiches, rolls, cakes and hot and cold drinks. In most bars you are required to go first to the cash desk, make your order, pay and get a receipt (**scontrino**) which you then hand to the barman and repeat your order. You will notice that most Italians stand up in bars – sitting down costs extra. The sign **tavola calda** means that hot dishes are also served.

For full meals there are **osteria**, **pizzeria**, **trattoria**, **taverna** and **ristorante**. Wherever possible, it's a good idea to choose the **menu turistico** (tourist menu) or the **menu fisso** (set menu). Although the variety is more restricted, the food is of the same standard and you get a good deal more for your money, without having to face any service charge shocks at the end of the meal. Always ask for the local culinary specialities and local wine as they are generally excellent, and wine is a great deal cheaper and of superior quality in its place of origin.

In Italy, you can order the following types of coffee: **espresso** – strong black coffee; **caffè macchiato** – espresso with a dash of milk; **cappuccino** – frothy, milky coffee sprinkled with cocoa; **caffelatte** – white coffee. These are the most common but you also get **caffè corretto** – **espresso** with a liqueur; **caffè decaffeinato** – decaffeinated coffee; **caffè lungo** – weak **espresso**; **caffè ristretto** – strong **espresso**. Remember that if you ask for: 'Un caffè, per favore', you will be served an **espresso**.

USEFUL WORDS AND PHRASES

beer	la birra	_beer-ra_
bill	il conto	_konto_
bottle	la bottiglia	_bot-teel-ya_
bread	il pane	_panay_
butter	il burro	_boor-ro_

café	il caffè	*kaf-feh*
cake	la torta	*torta*
carafe	la caraffa	*karaf-fa*
children's portion	una porzione per bambini	*portz-yonay pair bambeenee*
coffee	il caffè	*kaf-feh*
cup	la tazza	*tatza*
dessert	il dessert	*'dessert'*
fork	la forchetta	*forket-ta*
glass	il bicchiere	*beek-yairay*
half-litre	da mezzo litro	*da metzo leetro*
knife	il coltello	*koltel-lo*
litre	un litro	*leetro*
main course	il piatto principale	*p-yat-to preencheepalay*
menu	il menù	*maynoo*
milk	il latte	*lat-tay*
pepper	il pepe	*paypay*
plate	il piatto	*p-yat-to*
receipt *(in bars)*	lo scontrino	*skontreeno*
(in restaurants)	la ricevuta	*reechevoota*
restaurant	il ristorante	*reestorantay*
salt	il sale	*salay*
sandwich	il panino	*paneeno*
serviette	il tovagliolo	*toval-yolo*
snack	lo spuntino	*spoonteeno*
soup	la minestra	*meenestra*
spoon	il cucchiaio	*kook-ya-yo*
starter	l'antipasto	*anteepasto*
sugar	lo zucchero	*dzookairo*
table	il tavolo	*tavolo*
tea	il tè	*teh*
teaspoon	il cucchiaino	*kook-ya-eeno*
tip	la mancia	*mancha*
waiter	il cameriere	*kamair-yairay*
waitress	la cameriera	*kamair-yaira*
water	l'acqua	*akwa*

59

wine	il vino	*veeno*
wine list	la lista dei vini	*leesta day veenee*

A table for one/two/three please
Un tavolo per una persona/per due/per tre, per favore
oon tavolo pair oona pairsona/pair doo-ay/pair tray pair favoray

Can I see the menu/wine list?
Potrei vedere il menu/la lista dei vini?
potray vedairay eel maynoo/la leesta day veenee

What would you recommend?
Cosa ci consiglia?
koza chee konseel-ya

I'd like ...
Vorrei...
vor-ray

Just an espresso/cappuccino/white coffee, please
Solo un caffè/un cappuccino/un caffelatte, per favore
solo oon kaf-feh/oon kap-poocheeno/oon kaf-faylat-tay pair favoray

I only want a snack
Vorrei solo uno spuntino
vor-ray solo oono spoonteeno

Is there a set menu?
C'è un menù fisso?
cheh oon maynoo fees-so

Can we try a local speciality/wine?
Potremmo assaggiare una specialità/un vino locale?
potrem-mo as-saj-jaray oona spech-yaleeta/oon veeno lokalay

A litre of house red, please
Un litro di vino rosso della casa, per favore
oona leetro dee veeno ros-so del-la kaza pair favoray

60

Do you have any vegetarian dishes?
Avete piatti vegetariani?
avetay p-yat-tee vejetar-yanee

Could we have some water?
Potremmo avere un po' d'acqua?
potrem-mo avairay oon po dakwa

Is there a children's menu?
C'è un menù per bambini?
cheh oon maynoo pair bambeenee

Waiter/waitress!
Cameriere/cameriera!
kamair-yairay/kamair-yaira

We didn't order this!
Non lo abbiamo ordinato!
non lo abb-yamo ordeenato

You've forgotten to bring my dessert
Ha dimenticato di portarmi il dessert
a deementeekato dee portarmee eel 'dessert'

May we have some more ...?
Potremmo avere ancora un po' di...?
potrem-mo avairay ankora oon po dee

Can I have another knife/spoon?
Potrei avere un altro coltello/cucchiaio?
potray avairay oon altro koltel-lo/kook-ya-yo

Can we have the bill, please?
Può portarci il conto, per favore?
pwo portarchee eel konto pair favoray

Could I have a receipt, please?
Potrei avere la ricevuta/lo scontrino, per favore?
potray avairay la reechevoota/lo skontreeno pair favoray

Can we pay separately?
Possiamo pagare separatamente?
poss-yamo pagaray separatamentay

That was very good, thank you
Era ottimo, grazie
aira ot-teemo gratzee-ay

YOU MAY HEAR

Buon appetito!
Enjoy your meal!

Cosa vuole da bere?
What would you like to drink?

Avete mangiato bene?
Did you enjoy your meal?

---

abbacchio alla romana	Roman-style spring lamb
acciughe sott'olio	anchovies in oil
aceto	vinegar
acqua	water
acqua minerale gassata	sparkling mineral water
acqua minerale non gassata	still mineral water
acqua naturale	still mineral water, tap water
affettato misto	variety of cold, sliced meats such as salami, cooked ham etc
affogato al caffè	ice cream with hot *espresso* coffee poured over it
aglio	garlic
agnello	lamb
agnello al forno	roast lamb
albicocche	apricots
ananas	pineapple
anatra	duck
anatra all'arancia	duck in orange sauce
anguilla in umido	stewed eel
anguria	water melon
antipasti	starters
antipasti misti	variety of starters
aperitivo	aperitif
aragosta	lobster
arancia	orange
aranciata	orangeade
aringa	herring
arista di maiale al forno	roast chine of pork
arrosto di tacchino	roast turkey
arrosto di vitello	roast veal
asparagi	asparagus
avocado all'agro	avocado pears with oil and lemon or vinegar
baccalà	dried cod
baccalà alla vicentina	Vicentine-style dried cod
bagnacauda	vegetables (usually raw) in an oil, garlic and anchovy sauce
barbaresco	dry, red wine from the Piedmont region

barbera	dry red wine from Piedmont
bardolino	dry red wine from area around Verona
barolo	dark, dry red wine from Piedmont
basilico	basil
bavarese	ice-cream cake with cream
bel paese	soft, full-fat white cheese
besciamella	white sauce
bignè	cream puff
birra	beer
birra chiara	light beer, lager
birra grande	large beer *(approx. 1 pint)*
birra piccola	small beer *(approx. $\frac{1}{2}$ pint)*
birra scura	dark beer
bistecca (di manzo)	beef steak
bistecca ai ferri	grilled steak
bollito misto	assorted boiled meats with vegetables
braciola di maiale	pork steak
branzino al forno	baked sea bass
brasato	braised beef with herbs
bresaola	dried, salted beef sliced thinly and eaten cold with oil and lemon
brioche	type of croissant
brodo	clear broth
brodo di pollo	chicken broth
brodo vegetale	clear, vegetable broth
budino	pudding
burro	butter
burro di acciughe	anchovy butter
caciotta	tender, white, medium-fat cheese from Central Italy
caffè	coffee
caffè corretto	*espresso* coffee with a dash of liqueur
caffè lungo	weak *espresso* coffee
caffè macchiato	*espresso* coffee with a dash of milk
caffè ristretto	strong *espresso* coffee
caffellatte	half coffee, half hot milk
calamari in umido	stewed squid
calamaro	squid
calzone	folded pizza with tomato and mozzarella or *ricotta* inside

camomilla	camomile tea
cannella	cinnamon
cannelloni al forno	rolls of egg pasta stuffed with meat and baked in the oven
cappelle di funghi porcini alla griglia	grilled boletus mushroom caps
cappuccino	*espresso* coffee with foaming milk and a sprinkling of cocoa powder
capretto al forno	roast kid
carciofi	artichokes
carciofini sott'olio	baby artichokes in oil
carne	meat
carote	carrots
carpaccio	finely-sliced beef fillets with oil, lemon and grated parmesan
carré di maiale al forno	roast pork loin
cassata siciliana	Sicilian ice-cream cake with glacé fruit, chocolate and *ricotta*
castagne	chestnuts
cavoletti di Bruxelles	Brussels sprouts
cavolfiore	cauliflower
cavolo	cabbage
cefalo	mullet
cernia	grouper *(fish)*
charlotte	ice-cream cake with milk, eggs, cream, biscuits and fruit
chianti	dark red Tuscan wine
ciambella	ring-shaped cake
cicoria	chicory
cicorino	small chicory plants
ciliege	cherries
cime di rapa	young leaves of turnip plant
cioccolata	chocolate
cioccolata calda	hot chocolate
cipolle	onions
cocktail di gamberetti	prawn cocktail
conchiglie alla marchigiana	pasta shells in tomato sauce with celery, carrot, parsley and ham
coniglio	rabbit
coniglio arrosto	roast rabbit
coniglio in salmí	jugged rabbit

coniglio in umido	stewed rabbit
consommé	clear broth made with meat or chicken
contorni	vegetables
coperto	cover charge
coppa	cured neck of pork, sliced finely and eaten cold
costata alla fiorentina	Florentine entrecôte
costata di manzo	beef entrecôte
cotechino	spiced pork sausage for boiling
cotoletta	veal, pork or lamb chop
cotoletta ai ferri	grilled veal or pork chop
cotoletta alla milanese	veal chop in breadcrumbs
cotoletta alla valdostana	veal chop with ham and cheese cooked in breadcrumbs
cotolette di agnello	lamb chops
cotolette di maiale	pork chops
cozze	mussels
cozze alla marinara	mussels in seafood sauce
crema	custard dessert made with eggs and milk
crema al caffè	coffee custard dessert
crema al cioccolato	chocolate custard dessert
crema di funghi	cream of mushroom soup
crema di piselli	cream of pea soup
crema pasticciera	confectioner's custard
crêpe suzette	pancake flambéed with orange sauce
crescente	type of flat, fried Emilian bread made with flour, lard and eggs
crespelle	type of savoury pancake filled with white sauce and other fillings
crespelle ai funghi	savoury pancakes with mushrooms
crespelle al formaggio	savoury pancakes with cheese
crespelle al pomodoro	savoury pancakes with tomato
crostata di frutta	fruit tart
dadi	stock cubes
datteri	dates
degustazione	tasting
degustazione di vini	wine tasting
denominazione di origine controllata (DOC)	guarantee of quality of wine

dentice al forno	baked dentex *(type of sea bream)*
digestivo	digestive liqueur
dolci	sweets, desserts, cakes
endivia belga	Belgian endives
entrecôte (di manzo)	beef entrecôte
espresso	strong black coffee
fagiano	pheasant
fagioli	beans
fagioli borlotti in umido	fresh borlotti beans *(type of kidney bean)* cooked in vegetables, herbs and tomato sauce
fagiolini	long, green beans
faraona	guinea fowl
fegato	liver
fegato alla veneta	liver cooked in butter with onions
fegato con salvia e burro	liver cooked in butter and sage
fettuccine	ribbon-shaped pasta
fettuccine al salmone	*fettuccine* with salmon
fettuccine panna e funghi	*fettuccine* with cream and mushrooms
fichi	figs
filetti di pesce persico	fillets of perch
filetti di sogliola	fillets of sole
filetto (di manzo)	fillet of beef
filetto ai ferri	grilled fillet of beef
filetto al cognac	fillet of beef in cognac
filetto al pepe verde	fillet of beef with green pepper
filetto al sangue	rare fillet of beef
filetto ben cotto	well-done fillet of beef
filetto medio	medium fillet of beef
finocchio	fennel
finocchi gratinati	fennel with melted, grated cheese
fonduta	cheese fondue
formaggi misti	variety of cheeses
fragole	strawberries
fragole con gelato/panna	strawberries and ice cream/cream
frappé	whisked fruit or milk drink with crushed ice
frappé al cioccolato	chocolate milk shake
frascati	dry, white wine from area around Rome
frittata	type of omelette

frittata al formaggio	cheese omelette
frittata al prosciutto	ham omelette
frittata alle erbe	herb omelette
frittata alle verdure	vegetable omelette
fritto misto	mixed seafood in batter
frittura di pesce	variety of fried fish
frutta	fruit
frutta alla fiamma	fruit flambé
frutta secca	dried nuts and raisins
frutti di bosco	mixture of strawberries, raspberries, mulberries etc
frutti di mare	seafood
funghi	mushrooms
funghi trifolati	mushrooms fried in garlic and parsley
gamberetti	shrimps
gamberi	prawns
gamberoni	king prawns
gazzosa	clear lemonade
gelatina	gelatine
gelato	ice cream
gelato con panna	ice cream with cream
gelato di crema	vanilla-flavoured ice cream
gelato di frutta	fruit-flavoured ice cream
gnocchetti verdi agli spinaci e al gorgonzola	small flour, potato and spinach dumplings with melted gorgonzola
gnocchi	small flour and potato dumplings
gnocchi alla romana	small milk and semolina dumplings baked with butter
gnocchi al pomodoro	small flour and potato dumplings in tomato sauce
gorgonzola	strong, soft blue cheese from Lombardy
grancevola	spiny spider crab
granchio	crab
granita	drink with crushed ice
granita di caffè	iced coffee
granita di caffè con panna	iced coffee with cream
granita di limone	lemon drink with crushed ice
grigliata di pesce	grilled fish
grigliata mista	mixed grill *(meat or fish)*
grissini	thin, crisp breadsticks

gruviera	Gruyère cheese
indivia	endive
insalata	salad
insalata caprese	salad of sliced tomatoes and mozzarella
insalata di funghi porcini	boletus mushroom salad
insalata di mare	seafood salad
insalata di nervetti	boiled beef or veal served cold with beans and pickles
insalata di pomodori	tomato salad
insalata di riso	rice salad
insalata mista	mixed salad
insalata russa	Russian salad
insalata verde	green salad
involtini	meat rolls stuffed with ham and herbs
lamponi	raspberries
lamponi con gelato/panna	raspberries and ice cream/cream
lasagne al forno	layers of thick, flat pasta baked in tomato sauce, mince and cheese
latte	milk
latte macchiato con cioccolato	hot, foamy milk with a sprinkling of cocoa powder
lattuga	lettuce
leggero	light
legumi	pulses
lemonsoda	sparkling lemon drink
lenticchie	lentils
lepre	hare
limonata	lemon-flavoured fizzy drink
limone	lemon
lingua	tongue
lingua salmistrata	ox tongue marinaded in brine and then cooked
macedonia di frutta	fruit salad
macedonia di frutta al maraschino	fruit salad in Maraschino
macedonia di frutta con gelato	fruit salad with ice cream
maiale	pork
maionese	mayonnaise
mandarino	mandarin
mandorla	almond

manzo	beef
marroni	chestnuts
marsala	very sweet wine similar to sherry
marzapane	marzipan
medaglioni di vitello	veal medallions
mela	apple
melanzane	aubergines
melanzane alla siciliana	baked aubergine slices with parmesan, tomato sauce and egg
melone	melon
menta	mint
menu turistico	tourist menu
meringata	meringue pie
meringhe con panna	meringues with cream
merlot	dark red wine of French origin
merluzzo	cod
merluzzo alla pizzaiola	cod in tomato sauce with anchovies, capers and parsley
merluzzo in bianco	boiled cod with oil and lemon
messicani in gelatina	rolls of veal in gelatine
millefoglie	layered pastry slice with confectioners' custard
minestra in brodo	noodle soup
minestrone	thick vegetable soup with rice or *vermicelli*
mirtilli	bilberries
mirtilli con gelato/panna	bilberries and ice cream/cream
more	mulberries or blackberries
more con gelato/panna	mulberries or blackberries and ice cream/cream
moscato	sweet, sparkling wine
mostarda di Cremona	preserve of glacé fruit in grape must or sugar with syrup and mustard
mousse al cioccolato	chocolate mousse
mozzarella	firm, white, milky buffalo cheese
mozzarella in carrozza	slices of bread and mozzarella coated in flour and fried
nasello	hake
noce moscata	nutmeg
nocciole	hazelnuts
noci	walnuts

nodino	veal chop
olio	oil
orata al forno	baked gilthead *(fish)*
origano	oregano
ossobuco	stewed shin of veal
ostriche	oysters
paglia e fieno	mixture of plain and green *tagliatelle*
paillard di manzo	slices of grilled beef
paillard di vitello	slices of grilled veal
pane	bread
panino	filled roll
panna	cream
parmigiana di melanzane	baked dish of aubergines, tomato sauce, mozzarella and parmesan
parmigiano	parmesan cheese
pasta al forno	pasta baked in white sauce and grated cheese
pasta e fagioli	very thick soup with puréed borlotti beans and small pasta rings
pasta e piselli	pasta with peas
pasticcio di fegato d'oca	baked, pasta-covered dish with goose liver
pasticcio di lepre	baked, pasta-covered dish with hare
pasticcio di maccheroni	baked macaroni
pastina in brodo	noodle soup
patate	potatoes
patate al forno	baked potatoes
patate arrosto	roast potatoes
patate fritte	chips
patate in insalata	potato salad
pâté di carne	pâté
pâté di fegato	liver pâté
pâté di pesce	fish pâté
pecorino	strong, hard ewe's milk cheese
penne	pasta quills
penne ai quattro formaggi	pasta quills with sauce made from four cheeses
penne all'arrabbiata	pasta quills with tomato and chilli pepper sauce
penne panna e prosciutto	pasta quills with cream and ham sauce

pepe	pepper *(spice)*
peperoni	peppers
peperoni ripieni	stuffed peppers
peperoni sott'olio	peppers in oil
pera	pear
pesca	peach
pesca melba	peach melba
pesce	fish
pesce al cartoccio	fish baked in foil with herbs
pesce in carpione	marinaded fish
pinot	dry white wine from the Veneto region
pinzimonio	assorted whole, raw vegetables eaten with oil and vinegar
piselli	peas
piselli al prosciutto	fresh peas cooked in clear broth, butter, ham and basil
pizza Margherita	pizza with tomato and mozzarella
pizza napoletana	pizza with tomato, mozzarella and anchovies
pizza quattro stagioni	pizza with tomato, mozzarella, ham, mushrooms and artichokes
pizzaiola	slices of cooked beef in tomato sauce, oregano and anchovies
pizzoccheri alla Valtellinese	thin, pasta strips with green vegetables, melted butter and cheese
polenta	yellow cornmeal boiled in water with salt, then left to set and cut in slices
polenta e funghi	*polenta* with mushrooms
polenta e latte	*polenta* with milk
polenta e osei	*polenta* with small birds
polenta pasticciata	alternate layers of *polenta*, tomato sauce and cheese
pollo	chicken
pollo alla cacciatora	chicken in white wine and mushroom sauce
pollo alla diavola	chicken pieces flattened and deep-fried
pollo al forno/arrosto	roast chicken
polpette	meatballs
polpettone	meatloaf

pomodori	tomatoes
pomodori ripieni	stuffed tomatoes
pompelmo	grapefruit
porri	leeks
prezzemolo	parsley
primi piatti	first courses
prosciutto cotto	cooked ham
prosciutto crudo/di Parma	type of cured ham
prosciutto di Praga	cooked ham
prosciutto e fichi	cured ham with figs
prosciutto e melone	cured ham with melon
prugne	plums
punte di asparagi all'agro	asparagus tips in oil and lemon
purè di patate	creamed potatoes
quaglie	quails
radicchio	chicory
ragù	sauce made with mince, tomatoes and diced vegetables
rapa	type of white turnip with flavour similar to radish
rapanelli	radishes
ravioli	small, square-shaped egg pasta filled with meat or cheese
ravioli al pomodoro	ravioli stuffed with meat, in tomato sauce
razza	skate
ricotta	type of cottage cheese
risi e bisi	*risotto* with peas and small pieces of ham
riso	rice
riso al pomodoro	rice with tomato
riso in brodo	rice in clear broth
riso in insalata	rice salad
risotto	rice cooked in stock
risotto ai funghi	mushroom *risotto*
risotto al nero di seppia	black *risotto* made with cuttlefish ink
risotto al salmone	salmon *risotto*
risotto al tartufo	truffle *risotto*
risotto alla castellana	*risotto* with mushroom, ham, cream and cheese sauce
risotto alla milanese	*risotto* flavoured with saffron

roast-beef all'inglese	roast beef (sliced very thinly and served cold with lemon)
robiola	type of soft cheese from Lombardy
rognone trifolato	small kidney pieces in garlic, oil and parsley
rosatello/rosato	rosé wine
rosmarino	rosemary
salame	salami
sale	salt
salmone affumicato	smoked salmon
salsa cocktail	mayonnaise and ketchup sauce for garnishing fish and seafood
salsa di pomodoro	tomato sauce
salsa tartara	tartar sauce
salsa vellutata	white sauce made with clear broth instead of milk
salsa verde	sauce for meats made with chopped parsley and oil
salsiccia	sausage
salsiccia di cinghiale	wild boar sausage
salsiccia di maiale	pork sausage
saltimbocca alla romana	slices of veal rolled with ham and sage and fried
salvia	sage
sambuca (con la mosca)	aniseed-flavour liqueur from Lazio region served with a coffee bean in the glass
sarde ai ferri	grilled sardines
scaloppine	veal escalopes
scaloppine ai carciofi	veal escalopes with artichokes
scaloppine ai funghi	veal escalopes with mushrooms
scaloppine al Marsala	veal escalopes in Marsala
scaloppine al prezzemolo	veal escalopes with parsley
scaloppine al vino bianco	veal escalopes in white wine
scamorza alla griglia	grilled soft cheese
scampi alla griglia	grilled scampi
secco	dry
secondi piatti	second courses, main courses
sedano di Verona	Veronese celery
selvaggina	game
semifreddo	dessert made of ice cream and sponge

senape	mustard
seppie in umido	stewed cuttlefish
servizio compreso	service charge included
servizio escluso	not including service charge
soave	dry white wine from region around Lake Garda
sogliola	sole
sogliola ai ferri	grilled sole
sogliola al burro	sole cooked in butter
sogliola alla mugnaia	sole cooked in flour and butter
sorbetto	sorbet, soft ice cream
soufflé al formaggio	cheese soufflé
soufflé al prosciutto	ham soufflé
spaghetti	spaghetti
spaghetti aglio, olio e peperoncino	spaghetti with garlic, oil and crushed chilli pepper
spaghetti al pesto	spaghetti in crushed basil, garlic, oil and parmesan dressing
spaghetti al pomodoro	spaghetti in tomato sauce
spaghetti al ragù	spaghetti with mince and tomato sauce
spaghetti alla carbonara	spaghetti with egg, chopped bacon and cheese sauce
spaghetti alla puttanesca	spaghetti with anchovies, capers and black olives in tomato sauce
spaghetti alle vongole	spaghetti with clams
spaghetti all'matriciana	spaghetti in minced pork and tomato sauce typical of Rome
speck	type of cured, smoked ham
spezzatino di vitello	veal stew
spiedini	small pieces of assorted meats or fish cooked on a spit
spinaci	spinach
spinaci all'agro	spinach with oil and lemon
spremuta d'arancia	freshly squeezed orange juice
spremuta di limone	freshly squeezed lemon juice
spumante	sparkling wine
stracchino	type of soft cheese from Lombardy
stracciatella	beaten eggs cooked in boiling, clear broth
strudel di mele	apple strudel

succo d'arancia	orange juice
succo di albicocca	apricot juice
succo di pera	pear juice
succo di pesca	peach juice
succo di pompelmo	grapefruit juice
sugo al tonno	tomato sauce with garlic, tuna and parsley
svizzera	hamburger
tacchino ripieno	stuffed turkey
tagliata	finely-cut beef fillet cooked in the oven
tagliatelle	thin, flat strips of egg pasta
tagliatelle al basilico	*tagliatelle* and chopped basil
tagliatelle alla bolognese	*tagliatelle* with mince and tomato sauce
tagliatelle al pomodoro	*tagliatelle* with tomato sauce
tagliatelle al ragù	*tagliatelle* with mince and tomato sauce
tagliatelle con panna e funghi	*tagliatelle* with cream and mushroom sauce
tagliatelle rosse	*tagliatelle* with chopped red peppers
tagliatelle verdi	*tagliatelle* with chopped spinach
tagliolini	thin, soup noodles
tagliolini ai funghi	*tagliolini* with mushrooms
tagliolini alla panna	*tagliolini* with cream
tagliolini al salmone	*tagliolini* with salmon
tartine	small sandwiches
tartufo	round ice cream covered in cocoa or chocolate
tè	tea
tè con latte	tea with milk
tè con limone	lemon tea
tiramisù	dessert made with coffee-soaked sponge, eggs, Marsala cream and cocoa powder
tonno	tuna
torta	tart, flan
torta salata	savoury flan
torta ai carciofi	artichoke flan
torta al cioccolato	chocolate tart
torta al formaggio	cheese flan

torta di mele	apple tart
torta di noci	walnut tart
torta di ricotta	type of cheesecake
torta di zucchine	courgette flan
torta gelato	ice-cream tart
tortellini	small pasta shapes filled with minced pork, ham, parmesan and nutmeg
tortellini alla panna	*tortellini* with cream
tortellini al pomodoro	*tortellini* with tomato sauce
tortellini al ragù	*tortellini* with mince and tomato sauce
tortellini in brodo	*tortellini* in clear broth
tortelloni di magro/di ricotta	pasta shapes filled with cheese, parsley, chopped vegetables
tortelloni di zucca	*tortelloni* stuffed with pumpkin
trancio di palombo	smooth hound slice *(fish)*
trancio di pesce spada	swordfish steak
trenette col pesto	type of flat spaghetti with crushed basil, garlic, oil and cheese sauce
triglie	mullet *(fish)*
trippa	tripe
trota	trout
trota affumicata	smoked trout
trota al burro	trout cooked in butter
trota alle mandorle	trout with almonds
trota bollita	boiled trout
uccelletti	small birds wrapped in bacon, served on cocktail sticks
uova	eggs
uova al tegamino con pancetta	fried eggs and bacon
uova alla coque	boiled eggs
uova farcite	eggs with tuna, capers and mayonnaise filling
uova sode	hard-boiled eggs
uva	grapes
uva bianca	white grapes
uva nera	black grapes
vellutata di asparagi	creamed asparagus with egg yolks
vellutata di piselli	creamed peas with egg yolks
verdura	vegetables
vermicelli	very fine, thin pasta, often used in soups

vino	wine
vino bianco	white wine
vino da dessert	dessert wine
vino da pasto	table wine
vino da tavola	table wine
vino rosso	red wine
vitello	veal
vitello tonnato	sliced veal in blended tuna, anchovy, oil and lemon sauce
vongole	clams
würstel	frankfurter
zabaione	creamy dessert made from beaten eggs, sugar and Marsala
zafferano	saffron
zucca	pumpkin
zucchine	courgettes
zucchine al pomodoro	chopped courgettes in tomato, garlic and parsley sauce
zucchine ripiene	stuffed courgettes
zuccotto	ice-cream cake with sponge, cream and chocolate
zuppa	soup
zuppa di cipolle	onion soup
zuppa di cozze	mussel soup
zuppa di lenticchie	lentil soup
zuppa di pesce	fish soup
zuppa di verdura	vegetable soup
zuppa inglese	trifle

SHOPS AND SERVICES

This chapter covers all sorts of shopping needs and services, and to start with you'll find some general phrases which can be used in lots of different places – many of which are named in the list below. After the general phrases come some more specific requests and sentences to use when you've found what you need, be it food, clothing, repairs, film-developing, a haircut or haggling in the market. Don't forget to refer to the mini-dictionary for items you may be looking for.

Shops are usually open from 8.30/9 am to 12.30/1 pm and from 3.30/4 pm to 7.30/8 pm and often later in tourist resorts in the high season. Shop hours may vary slightly according to the region you are in and shops may close on different days of the week – often on Monday mornings, all day Monday or on Thursday afternoons. Venice has half-day closing (only in winter) on Monday mornings. In Florence, shops are closed on Monday mornings or all day Monday in winter, autumn and spring and are closed on Saturday afternoons in August. Most large shops and supermarkets are open Monday to Saturday.

It's acceptable to haggle in the market but only if the price is not displayed.

In Italy, **chili** (kilos) and **etti** (hectograms) are used. One **etto** = 100 grams. Cheese, ham etc are generally sold by the **etto** and fruit and vegetables by the kilo.

There are some differences between Italian and British shops. Chemists are very expensive (see HEALTH page 113). So if you should need items such as antiseptic, toothpaste, plasters, tampons etc then it's better to·go to a supermarket or to a **drogheria** (*drogairee-a*), which is like a chemist's and general grocery store combined. If you wish to buy perfumes or sophisticated cosmetic products, you should go to a **profumeria** (*profoomairee-a*). If you want to buy films or get your photos developed go to a photographic shop or an optician's, NOT to a chemist's.

In Italy you won't find the type of launderette where you can do your own washing and drying. A dry cleaner's will only accept clothes for dry-cleaning or large items such as bed linen, but not small personal items.

For cigarettes, stamps, chewing gum and postcards go to a **tabaccaio** which can be identified by a white **T** on a black background. A **tabaccaio** generally has the same opening hours as shops. After 7.30/8 pm, you can only buy cigarettes in specially licensed bars or in railway stations.

USEFUL WORDS AND PHRASES

antique shop	il negozio di antiquariato	*negotz-yo dee anteekwar-yato*
audio equipment shop	il negozio di hi-fi	*negotz-yo dee 'hi-fi'*
baker's	la panetteria	*panet-tairee-a*
boutique	la boutique	*booteek*
bookshop	la libreria	*leebrairee-a*
butcher's	la macelleria	*machel-lairee-a*
buy	comprare	*kompraray*
cake shop	la pasticceria	*pasteechairee-a*
camera shop	il negozio di macchine fotografiche	*negotz-yo dee mak-keenay fotografeekay*
camping equipment	l'attrezzatura da campeggio	*at-tretz-zatoora da kampej-jo*
carrier bag	il sacchetto	*sak-ket-to*
cheap	economico	*ekonomeeko*
chemist's	la farmacia	*farmachee-a*
china	la porcellana	*porchel-lana*
confectioner's	la pasticceria	*pasteech-chairee-a*
cost	costare	*kostaray*
craft shop	il negozio di artigianato	*negotz-yo dee arteejanato*
department store	il grande magazzino	*granday magatzeeno*
dry cleaner's	la lavanderia a secco, la tintoria	*lavandairee-a a sek-ko, teentoree-a*

80

electrical goods store	il negozio di articoli elettrici	*negotz-yo dee arteekolee elet-treechee*
expensive	caro, costoso	*karo, kostozo*
fishmonger's	la pescheria	*peskairee-a*
florist's	il negozio di fiori	*negotz-yo dee f-yoree*
food store	il negozio di generi alimentari	*negotz-yo dee jaynairee aleementaree*
fruit	la frutta	*froot-ta*
gift shop	il negozio di articoli da regalo	*negotz-yo dee arteekolee da raygalo*
greengrocer's	il negozio di frutta e verdura	*negotz-yo dee froot-ta ay verdoora*
grocer's	il negozio di alimentari	*negotz-yo dee aleementaree*
hairdresser's		
(men's)	barbiere	*barb-yairay*
(women's)	parrucchiere, acconciature	*par-rookk-yairay, ak-konchatooray*
hardware shop	la ferramenta	*fair-ramenta*
hypermarket	l'ipermercato	*eepairmairkato*
indoor market	il mercato coperto	*mairkato kopairto*
jeweller's	la gioielleria	*joyel-lairee-a*
ladies' wear	l'abbigliamento per signora	*ab-beel-yamento pair seen-yora*
market	il mercato	*mairkato*
menswear	l'abbigliamento da uomo	*ab-beel-yamento da wommo*
newsagent's	la rivendita di giornali	*reevendeeta dee jornalee*
optician's	il negozio di ottica	*negotz-yo dee ot-teeka*
pharmacy	la farmacia	*farmachee-a*
receipt	lo scontrino	*skontreeno*
record shop	il negozio di dischi	*negotz-yo dee deeskee*
sale	la svendita, i saldi	*zvendeeta, saldee*
shoe repairer's	la calzoleria	*kaltzolairee-a*
shoe shop	il negozio di scarpe	*negotz-yo dee skarpay*
shop	il negozio	*negotz-yo*

souvenir shop	il negozio di souvenir	*negotz-yo dee sooveneer*
sports equipment	l'attrezzatura sportiva	*at-tretz-zatoora sporteeva*
sportswear	l'abbigliamento sportivo	*ab-beel-yamento sporteevo*
stationer's	la cartoleria	*kartolairee-a*
supermarket	il supermercato	*soopairmairkato*
tailor	il sarto	*sarto*
till	la cassa	*kas-sa*
tobacconist's	la tabaccheria	*tabak-kairee-a*
toyshop	il negozio di giocattoli	*negotz-yo dee jokat-tolee*
travel agent's	l'agenzia di viaggio	*ajentzee-a dee vee-aj-jo*
vegetables	la verdura	*vairdoora*
wine merchant's	la bottiglieria	*bot-teel-yairee-a*

Excuse me, where is/where are ...?
Mi scusi, dov'è/dove sono...?
mee skoozee doveh/dovay sono

Where is there a ... (shop)?
Dov'è un negozio di... qui vicino?
doveh oon negotz-yo dee ... kwee veecheeno

Where is the ... department?
Dov'è il reparto...?
doveh eel reparto

Where is the main shopping area?
Dov'è la zona dei negozi?
doveh la zona day negotzi

Is there a market here?
C'è un mercato qui?
cheh oon mairkato kwee

I'd like ...
Vorrei...
vor-ray

Do you have ...?
Avete...?
avaytay

How much is this?
Quanto costa questo?
kwanto kosta kwesto

Where do I pay?
Dove si paga?
dovay see paga

Do you take credit cards?
Accettate carte di credito?
ach-chet-tatay kartay dee kraydeeto

I think perhaps you've short-changed me
Penso che abbiate sbagliato di darmi il resto
penso kay abb-yatay sbal-yato dee darmee eel resto

Can I have a receipt/a bag, please?
Potrebbe darmi lo scontrino/un sacchetto?
potrayb-bay darmee lo skontreeno/oon sak-ket-to

I'm just looking
Sto solo dando un'occhiata
sto solo dando oon okk-yata

I'll come back later
Tornerò più tardi
tornairo p-yoo tardee

Do you have any more of these?
Ne ha ancora di questi?
nay a ankora dee kwestee

Have you anything cheaper?
Non ha niente di più economico?
non a n-yentay dee p-yoo ekonomeeko

Have you anything larger/smaller?
Non ne ha uno più grande/piccolo?
non nay a oono p-yoo granday/peek-kolo

Can I try it/them on?
Posso provarlo/provarli?
pos-so provarlo/provarlee

Does it come in other colours?
C'è anche in altri colori?
cheh ankay een altree koloree

Could you gift-wrap it for me?
Può farmi un pacchetto regalo?
pwo farmee oon pak-ket-to raygalo

I'd like to exchange this, it's faulty
Vorrei cambiare questo: è difettoso
vor-ray kamb-yaray kwesto: eh deefet-tozo

I'm afraid I don't have the receipt
Mi dispiace, ma non ho lo scontrino
mee deesp-yachay ma non oh lo skontreeno

Can I have a refund?
Posso riavere indietro i soldi?
pos-so ree-avairay endee-aytro ee soldee

My camera isn't working
La mia macchina fotografica non funziona
la mee-a mak-keena fotografeeka non foontz-yona

I want a 36-exposure colour film. 100ISO
Vorrei una pellicola 100ISO a colori da 36 foto
vor-ray oona pel-leekola 100 ee-ess-oh a koloree da 36 foto

I'd like this film processed
Vorrei sviluppare questa pellicola
vor-ray sveeloop-paray kwesta pel-leekola

Matt/glossy prints
Fotografie su carta opaca/lucida
fotografee-ay soo karta opaka/loocheeda

One-hour service, please
Vorrei il servizio in un'ora, per favore
vor-ray eel serveetz-yo een oon ora pair favoray

Where can I get this mended?
Dove posso farlo riparare?
dovay pos-so farlo reepararay

Can you mend this?
Può aggiustarmelo?
pwo aj-joostarmaylo

I'd like this skirt/these trousers dry-cleaned
Vorrei far pulire questa gonna/questi pantaloni
vor-ray far pooleeray kwesta gon-na/kwestee pantalonee

When will it/they be ready?
Quando sarà pronto/saranno pronti?
kwando sara pronto/saran-no prontee

I'd like to make an appointment
Vorrei prendere un appuntamento
vor-ray prendairay oon ap-poontamento

I want a cut and blow-dry
Vorrei taglio e messa in piega (con il föhn)
vor-ray tal-yo ay mes-sa een p-yayga kon eel fon

With conditioner/No conditioner, thanks
Con il balsamo/Senza il balsamo, grazie
kon eel bal-samo/sentza eel bal-samo gratzee-ay

85

Just a trim, please
Solo una spuntatina, per favore
solo oona spoontateena pair favoray

Not too much off!
Non tagli troppo!
non tal-yee trop-po

When does the market open?
Quando apre il mercato?
kwando apray eel mairkato

What's the price per kilo?
Quanto costa al chilo?
kwanto kosta al keelo

Could you write that down?
Può scriverlo?
pwo skreevairlo

That's too much! I'll pay …
È troppo! Lo do…
eh trop-po! lo do

Could I have a discount?
Potrebbe farmi uno sconto?
potrayb-bay farmee oono skonto

That's fine. I'll take it
Va bene. Lo prendo!
va baynay. lo prendo

I'll have a piece of that cheese
Vorrei un pezzo di quel formaggio
vor-ray oon petz-zo dee kwel formaj-jo

About 250/500 grams
Circa duecentocinquanta/cinquecento grammi
cheerka doo-ay-chentocheenkwanta/cheenkwaychento gram-mee

A kilo/half a kilo of apples, please
Un chilo/mezzo chilo di mele, per favore
oon keelo/metzo keelo dee maylay pair favoray

250 grams of that cheese, please
Due etti e mezzo di quel formaggio, per favore
doo-ay et-tee ay metzo dee kwel formaj-jo pair favoray

May I taste it?
Posso assaggiarlo?
pos-so as-saj-jarlo

That's very nice, I'll take some
Quello è molto buono; ne prenderò un po'
kwel-lo eh molto bwono; nay prayndairo oon po

It isn't what I wanted
Non è quello che volevo
non eh kwel-lo kay volayvo

THINGS YOU'LL SEE

abbigliamento da uomo	men's clothing
abbigliamento per signora	ladies' clothing
acconciature	ladies' hairdresser
agenzia di viaggio	travel agency
alimentari	groceries
barbiere	barber's
calzature	shoes
cartoleria	stationer's
cassa	cash desk, till
coiffeur	hair stylist
colpi di sole	highlights
dolci	confectionery, cakes
dozzina	dozen
elettrodomestici	electrical appliances
entrata	way in

→

87

fai-da-te	DIY
fioraio	flower shop
forniture per ufficio	office supplies
fresco	fresh
giocattoli	toys
grande magazzino	department store
la merce venduta non si cambia senza lo scontrino	goods are not exchanged without a receipt
libreria	bookshop
liquori	spirits
macelleria	butcher's
messa in piega con il föhn	blow-dry
moda	fashion
munitevi di un carrello/cestino	please take a trolley/basket
pagare alla cassa	pay at the desk
panetteria	bakery
parrucchiere (per signora)	ladies' hairdresser
pasticceria	cake shop
pellicceria	furrier
permanente	perm
pescheria	fish market
piano superiore	upper floor
prezzo	price
prima qualità	high quality
reparto	department
ribassato/ridotto	reduced
riviste	magazines
saldi	sales
salone da parrucchiere	hairdressing salon
salone per uomo	men's hairdresser
sartoria	tailor's
spingere	push
spuntata	trim
svendita	sale
tabacchi	tobacco

→

taglio	cut
tirare	pull
uscita	exit
verdure	vegetables

THINGS YOU'LL HEAR

Desidera?
Can I help you?

La stanno servendo?
Are you being served?

Non ha spiccioli?
Haven't you anything smaller? *(money)*

Mi dispiace quest'articolo è esaurito
I'm sorry, we're out of stock

Questo è tutto quello che abbiamo
This is all we have

Ha spiccioli/moneta?
Do you have any change?

Diamo solamente buoni acquisto
We only give credit notes

Si accomodi alla cassa, prego
Please pay at the till

Niente altro?
Will there be anything else?

Quanto ne vuole?
How much would you like?

Come lo desidera?
How would you like it?

SPORT

Whether you enjoy sport as a passive spectator or as an active participant, Italy has a great deal to offer. The Italians are passionate football fans and the championships are played from September to May, with some international matches in June and July. Cycling is also a favourite Italian sport and the **Giro d'Italia** – the annual race round the peninsula – takes place during May and June.

Summer sports include fishing, golf, skin diving, swimming and tennis. There is no lack of fine beaches in Italy and most of them are well-managed and provide everything for the tourist's enjoyment. There are numerous windsurfing schools where you can take lessons and hire all the necessary equipment, from boards to wetsuits. One of the most notable areas for this sport is Lake Garda.

Italy is a haven for mountain climbers and hill-walkers who will delight in discovering the many beautiful Alpine and Apennine valleys unknown to the average tourist. For winter sports there are excellently equipped skiing resorts in the Dolomites and in the Piedmont and Lombardy regions of Northern Italy.

USEFUL WORDS AND PHRASES

athletics	l'atletica	*atlayteeka*
ball	la palla	*pal-la*
bicycle	la bicicletta	*beecheeklet-ta*
binding *(ski)*	l'attacco (degli sci)	*at-tak-ko del-yee shee*
cable car	la funivia	*fooneevee-a*
canoe/canoeing	la canoa	*kano-a*
chair lift	la seggiovia	*sej-jovee-a*
cross-country skiing	lo sci di fondo	*shee dee fondo*
cycling	il ciclismo	*cheekleezmo*
go cycling	andare in bicicletta	*andaray een beecheeklet-ta*
dive	tuffarsi	*toof-farsee*

diving board	il trampolino	*trampoleeno*
downhill skiing	lo sci da discesa	*shee da deeshayza*
fishing	la pesca	*peska*
fishing rod	la canna da pesca	*kan-na da peska*
flippers	le pinne	*peen-nay*
football *(sport)*	il calcio	*kalcho*
(ball)	il pallone	*pal-lonay*
football match	la partita di calcio	*parteeta dee kalcho*
game *(match)*	la partita	*parteeta*
goggles	la maschera	*maskaira*
golf course	il campo da golf	*kampo da 'golf'*
play golf	giocare a golf	*jokaray a 'golf'*
gymnastics	la ginnastica	*jeen-nasteeka*
hang-gliding	il deltaplano	*deltaplano*
harpoon	l'arpione	*arp-yonay*
hunting	la caccia	*kach-cha*
ice-hockey	l'hockey su ghiaccio	*'hockey' soo g-yach-cho*
mast	l'albero	*albairo*
mountaineering	l'alpinismo	*alpeeneezmo*
nursery slope	la pista per principianti	*peesta pair preencheep-yantee*
parascending	il parapendio	*parapendee-o*
oxygen bottles	le bombole di ossigeno	*bombolay dee os-seejeno*
pedal boat	il pedalò	*pedalo*
piste	la pista	*peesta*
racket	la racchetta	*rak-ket-ta*
ride	andare a cavallo	*andaray a kaval-lo*
riding	l'equitazione	*aykweetatz-yonay*
riding hat	il cappello da fantino	*kap-pel-lo da fanteeno*
rock climbing	la roccia	*roch-cha*
saddle	la sella	*sel-la*
sail	la vela	*vayla*
sailboard	il surf	*'surf'*
sailing	la vela	*vayla*
go sailing	fare vela	*faray vayla*
shooting range	il tiro a segno	*teero a sen-yo*

skate	pattinare	*pat-teengray*
skates	i pattini	*pat-teenee*
skating rink	la pista di pattinaggio	*peesta dee pateenaj-jo*
ski	sciare	*shee-aray*
ski boots	gli scarponi da sci	*skarponee da shee*
skiing	lo sci	*shee*
skin diving	l'immersione subacquea	*eem-mairsjonay soobakway-a*
ski pass	lo ski pass	*'ski pass'*
skis	gli sci	*shee*
skisticks	i bastoncini	*bastoncheenee*
ski tow	lo skilift	*'skilift'*
ski trail	la pista da sci	*peesta da shee*
ski wax	la sciolina	*shee-oleena*
sledge	la slitta	*zleeta*
snorkel	il respiratore a tubo	*respeeratoray a toobo*
sports centre	il centro sportivo	*chentro sporteevo*
stadium	lo stadio	*stad-yo*
surfboard	il surf	*surf*
swim	nuotare	*nwotaray*
swimming pool	la piscina	*peesheena*
team	la squadra	*skwadra*
tennis court	il campo da tennis	*kampo da ten-nis*
toboggan	la slitta	*zleeta*
underwater fishing	la pesca subacquea	*peska soobakway-a*
volleyball	la pallavolo	*pal-lavolo*
water-ski	fare sci d'acqua	*faray shee dakwa*
water-skiing	lo sci d'acqua	*shee dakwa*
water-skis	gli sci d'acqua	*shee dakwa*
wet suit	la muta da sub	*moota da soob*
go windsurfing	praticare il windsurf	*prateekaray eel 'windsurf'*

How do I get to the beach?
Potrebbe indicarmi la strada per la spiaggia?
potrayb-bay eendeekarmee la strada pair la sp-yaj-ja

How deep is the water here?
Quant'è profonda qui l'acqua?
kwanteh profonda kwee lakwa

Is there an indoor/outdoor pool here?
C'è una piscina coperta/scoperta?
cheh oona peesheena kopairta/skopairta

Is it dangerous to swim here?
È pericoloso nuotare qui?
eh paireekolozo nwotaray kwee

Can I fish here?
Posso pescare qui?
pos-so peskaray kwee

Do I need a licence?
C'è bisogno della licenza?
cheh beezon-yo del-la leechentza

Is there a golf course near here?
C'è un campo da golf da queste parti?
cheh oon kampo da 'golf' da kwestay partee

Do I have to be a member?
È necessario essere socio?
eh neches-sar-yo es-sairay socho

Where can I hire ...?
Dove posso noleggiare...?
dovay pos-so nolej-jaray

I would like to hire a bike/some skis
Vorrei noleggiare una bicicletta/degli sci
vor-ray nolej-jaray oona beecheeklet-ta/del-yee shee

How much does it cost per hour/day?
Quanto costa all'ora/al giorno?
kwanto kosta al ora/al jorno

93

When does the lift start?
A che ora aprono gli impianti?
a kay ora aprono l-yee eemp-yantee

What are the snow conditions like today?
Quali sono le condizioni della neve oggi?
kwalee sono lay kondeetz-yonee del-la nayvay oj-jee

How much is a daily/weekly lift pass?
Quanto costa un abbonamento giornaliero/settimanale?
kwanto kosta oon ab-bonamento jornal-yairo/set-tee-manalay

I would like to take skiing lessons
Vorrei prendere lezioni di sci
vor-ray prendairay letz-yonee dee shee

Where are the nursery slopes?
Dove sono le discese per principianti?
dovay sono lay deeshayzay pair preencheep-yantee

Is it very steep?
È molto ripido?
eh molto reepeedo

I would like to take water-skiing lessons
Vorrei prendere lezioni di sci d'acqua
vor-ray prendairay letz-yonee dee shee dakwa

There's something wrong with this binding
C'è qualcosa che non va in questo attacco
cheh kwalkoza kay non va een kwesto at-tak-ko

I haven't played this before
Non ho mai provato prima
non oh mi provato preema

Let's go skating/swimming
Andiamo a pattinare/sciare
and-yamo a pat-teenaray/shee-aray

What's the score?
A quanto sono?
a kwanto sono

Who won?
Chi ha vinto?
kee a veento

THINGS YOU'LL SEE

alla seggiovia	to the chair lift
correnti pericolose	dangerous currents
divieto di balneazione	no bathing
divieto di pesca	no fishing
funivia	cable car
noleggio barche	boat hire
noleggio biciclette	cycle hire
noleggio sci	ski hire
non dondolarsi	no swinging
pedoni	pedestrians
pericolo	danger
pericolo di valanghe	danger of avalanches
piscina coperta	indoor swimming pool
piscina scoperta	open-air swimming pool
pista ciclabile	cycle path
pista da fondo	cross-country ski track
pista facile/difficile	easy/difficult slope
pista per slitte	toboggan run
prepararsi a scendere	get ready to alight
pronto soccorso	first aid
sci di fondo	cross-country skiing
scuola di sci	ski school
trampolino	diving board; ski jump
vietato bagnarsi	no bathing
vietato pescare	no fishing
vietato tuffarsi	no diving

POST OFFICES AND BANKS

Main post offices are open from 8.15 am to 7 pm, while local offices generally close at 2 pm. Post boxes in Italy are generally red, although there are some yellow ones. Stamps can be bought at the post office or, more conveniently, at any **tabaccaio** (tobacconist's). These are easily identifiable by the sign displayed outside – a white **T** on a black background.

Banks are open from 8.30 am to 1.30 pm and from 2.45 pm to 3.45 pm, from Monday to Friday. Generally speaking, it is better to change money in a bank than in a bureau de change (called **cambio** or **cambiavalute**), because the latter charge a commission. Bureaux de change are to be found in airports, in railway stations and in the city centre. In larger cities, you will find automatic bureaux de change with cash dispensers outside some banks.

You will find cash dispensers for Eurocheques and for credit cards outside the main banks (but a commission of about 5% is charged if you draw money with a credit card). Major credit cards are generally accepted in hotels, restaurants and shops, but not always. Small shops or restaurants do not accept them.

The Italian currency is the **lira** (plural **lire**, abbreviation **L.**). There are coins of 10, 20, 50, 100, 200 and 500 lire, and banknotes of 1,000, 2,000, 5,000, 10,000, 50,000 and 100,000 lire.

USEFUL WORDS AND PHRASES

airmail	la posta aerea	p_o_sta a-_ai_ray-a
bank	la banca	b_a_nka
banknote	la banconota	bankon_o_ta
cash	il denaro	den_a_ro
cash dispenser	lo sportello automatico	sport_e_l-lo owtom_a_teeko
change	cambiare	kamb-y_a_ray
cheque	l'assegno	as-s_e_n-yo

cheque book	il libretto degli assegni	*leebret-to del-yee as-sen-yee*
collection	la levata	*levata*
counter	lo sportello	*sportel-lo*
credit card	la carta di credito	*karta dee kraydeeto*
customs form	il modulo per la dogana	*modoolo pair la dogana*
delivery	la consegna	*konsen-ya*
deposit *(noun)*	il deposito	*daypozeeto*
(verb)	depositare	*daypozeetaray*
envelope	la busta	*boosta*
exchange rate	il tasso di cambio	*tas-so dee kam-bee-o*
fax *(noun)*	il fax	*'fax'*
(verb: document)	spedire via fax	*spedeeray vee-a 'fax'*
fax machine	il fax	*'fax'*
form	il modulo	*modoolo*
international money order	il vaglia postale internazionale	*val-ja postalay eentairnatz-yonalay*
letter	la lettera	*let-taira*
mail	la posta	*posta*
money order	il vaglia postale	*val-ja postalay*
package/parcel	il pacchetto, il pacco	*pak-ket-to, pak-ko*
post *(noun)*	la posta	*posta*
(verb)	spedire	*spedeeray*
postage rates	le tariffe postali	*tareef-fay postalee*
postal order	il vaglia postale	*val-ya postalay*
post box	la cassetta delle lettere	*cas-set-ta del-lay let-tairay*
postcard	la cartolina	*kartoleena*
postcode	il codice di avviamento postale	*kodeechay dee avv-yamento postalay*
poste-restante	fermo posta	*fairmo posta*
postman	il postino	*posteeno*
post office	l'ufficio postale	*oof-feecho postalay*
pound sterling	la lira sterlina	*leera stairleena*
registered letter	la raccomandata	*rak-komandata*
stamp	il francobollo	*frankobol-lo*

surface mail	la posta ordinaria	*posta ordeenaree-a*
telegram	il telegramma	*telegram-ma*
traveller's cheque	il traveller's cheque	*'traveller's cheque'*
withdraw	prelevare	*praylevaray*
withdrawal	il prelievo	*praylyayvvo*

How much is a postcard to England?
Quanto costa spedire una cartolina in Inghilterra?
kwanto kosta spedeeray oona kartoleena een eengeeltair-ra

I would like three 750-lira stamps
Vorrei tre francobolli da settecentocinquanta lire
vor-ray tray frankobol-lee da set-tay-chentocheenkwanta leeray

I want to register this letter
Vorrei spedire questa lettera per raccomandata
vor-ray spedeeray kwesta let-taira pair rak-komandata

I want to send this parcel to Scotland
Vorrei spedire questo pacco in Scozia
vor-ray spedeeray kwesto pak-ko een skotz-ya

How long does the post to America take?
Quanto ci mette la posta per arrivare in America?
kwanto chee met-tay la posta pair ar-reevaray een amaireeka

Where can I post this?
Dove posso imbucarlo?
dovay pos-so eembookarlo

Is there any mail for me?
C'è posta per me?
cheh posta pair may

I'd like to send a telegram/a fax
Vorrei spedire un telegramma/un fax
vor-ray spedeeray oon telegram-ma/oon 'fax'

This is to go airmail
Deve essere spedito per via aerea
dayvay es-sairay spaydeeto pair vee-a a-airay-a

I'd like to change this into 10,000 lire notes
Vorrei cambiare in banconote da diecimila
vor-ray kamb-yaray een bankonotay da dee-aycheemeela

Can I cash these traveller's cheques?
Posso cambiare questi traveller's cheques?
pos-so kamb-yaray kwestee 'traveller's cheques'

What is the exchange rate for the pound?
Qual è il tasso di cambio della sterlina?
kwaleh eel tas-so dee kam-bee-o del-la stairleena

Can I draw cash using this credit card?
Posso fare un prelievo usando la carta di credito?
pos-so faray oon prayl-yayvo oozando la karta dee kraydeeto

I'd like it in 50,000 lire notes
Vorrei banconote da cinquantamila
vor-ray bankonotay da cheenkwantameela

Could you give me smaller notes?
Può darmi banconote di piccolo taglio?
pwo darmee bankonotay dee peek-kolo tal-yo

THINGS YOU'LL SEE

affrancatura	postage
affrancatura per l'estero	postage abroad
assicurata	insured mail
cambiavalute/cambio	bureau de change
cartolina	postcard

→

99

codice (di avviamento) postale	postcode
compilare	to fill in
conto corrente	current account
deposito	deposit
destinatario	addressee
espresso	express
fermo posta	poste restante
francobollo	stamp
indirizzo	address
lettera	letter
orario di apertura	opening hours
mittente	sender
pacchetto	package
posta	mail
posta aerea	airmail
prelievo	withdrawal
raccomandata	registered letter
riempire	to fill in
sportello	counter
sportello pacchi	parcels counter
tariffa	rate, charge
tariffa interna	inland postage
telegrammi	telegrams

TELEPHONES

Old telephone boxes can be operated with 100 and 200 lire pieces or **gettoni** – tokens each worth 200 lire. But they are being replaced with phones that take 100, 200, 500 lire and tokens or phonecards (costing 5,000 or 10,000 lire) which can be bought at tobacconists. You can also use **gettoni** as normal currency, so don't be alarmed if you receive one in your change when shopping. When you need **gettoni** you can ask for them in any bar. If you need to make a long-distance phone call it is better to go to an office of the Italian national telephone company, the **SIP**, or to the **ASST (Azienda Statale Servizi Telefonici)** which is a department of the main post office in Florence and Venice. Alternatively, you can ask in a bar if the barman has **un telefono a scatti** – you make your call first and are then charged for the number of units you have used.

To telephone the UK, dial 00 44 followed by the area code (but exclude the 0 which prefixes all UK area codes) and the number you want. To call a USA number, dial 001 followed by the area code and the subscriber's number.

The tones you'll hear when telephoning in Italy are:

Dialling tone: two tones, one short and one long, at regular intervals;
Ringing tone: one single, long tone at regular intervals;
Engaged and unobtainable: short rapid pips.

USEFUL WORDS AND PHRASES

call *(noun)*	la telefonata	*telefonata*
(verb)	telefonare	*telefonaray*
cardphone	il telefono a scheda	*telefono a skayda*
code	il prefisso	*prefees-so*
crossed line	l'interferenza	*eentairfairentza*
dial	fare il numero	*faray eel noomairo*
dialling tone	il segnale di libero	*sen-yalay dee leebairo*
emergency	l'emergenza	*emairjentza*

101

enquiries	il servizio informazioni telefoniche	*sairveetz-yo eenformatz-yonee telefoneekay*
extension	l'interno	*eentairno*
international call	la chiamata internazionale	*k-yamata eentairnatz-yonalay*
number	il numero	*noomairo*
operator	l'operatore	*opairatoray*
payphone	il telefono a gettoni	*telefono a jet-tonee*
phonecard	la scheda telefonica	*skayda telefoneeka*
receiver	il ricevitore	*reecheveetoray*
reverse charge call	la chiamata a carico del destinatario	*k-yamata a kareeko del desteenataree-o*
telephone	il telefono	*telefono*
telephone box	la cabina telefonica	*kabeena telefoneeka*
telephone directory	la guida telefonica	*gweeda telefoneeka*
wrong number	il numero sbagliato	*noomairo zbal-yato*

Where is the nearest phone box?
Dov'è la cabina telefonica più vicina?
doveh la kabeena telefoneeka p-yoo veecheena

Is there a telephone directory?
C'è una guida telefonica?
cheh oona gweeda telefoneeka

I would like the directory for Venice
Vorrei la guida telefonica di Venezia
vor-ray la gweeda telefoneeka dee venetz-ya

Can I call abroad from here?
Posso fare una telefonata internazionale da qua?
pos-so faray oona telefonata eentairnatz-yonalay da kwa

I would like to reverse the charges
La metta a carico del destinatario
la met-ta a kareeko del desteenataree-o

I would like a number in Rome
Ho bisogno del numero di un abbonato di Roma
oh beezon-yo del noomairo dee oon ab-bonato dee roma

Can you give me an outside line?
Può darmi una linea esterna?
pwo darmee oona leenay-a estairna

How do I get an outside line?
Come devo fare per avere una linea esterna?
komay dayvo faray pair avairay oona leenay-a estairna

Hello, this is Anna speaking
Pronto, sono Anna
pronto sono an-na

Is that Mario?
Parlo con Mario?
parlo kon mar-yo

Speaking
Sono io/ All'apparecchio
sono ee-o/al-lap-parek-kyo

I would like to speak to Paola
Vorrei parlare con Paola
vor-ray parlaray kon paola

Extension 34 please, please
Interno trentaquattro, per favore
eentairno trentakwat-tro pair favoray

Please tell him/her Marina called
Per cortesia, gli/le dica che ha telefonato Marina
pair kortezee-a l-yee/lay deeka kay a telefonato mareena

Ask him/her to call me back please
Gli/le dica di ritelefonarmi, per favore
l-yee/lay deeka dee reetelefonarmee pair favoray

My number is 753522
Il mio numero è sette cinque tre cinque due due
eel mee-o noomairo eh set-tay cheenkway tray cheenkway doo-ay doo-ay

Do you know where he/she is?
Non sa dov'è?
non sa doveh

When will he/she be back?
Quando tornerà?
kwando tornaira

Could you leave him/her a message?
Potrebbe lasciargli/lasciarle un messaggio?
potrayb-bay lasharl-yee/lasharlay oon mes-saj-jo

I'll ring back later
Ritelefonerò più tardi
reetelefonairo p-yoo tardee

Sorry, I've got the wrong number
Mi scusi, ho sbagliato numero
mee skoozee oh zbal-yato noomairo

You've got the wrong number
Ha sbagliato numero
a zbal-yato noomairo

THE ALPHABET

a	*ah*	h	*ak-ka*	o	*o*	v	*voo*
b	*bee*	i	*ee*	p	*pee*	w	*voo dopp-yo*
c	*chee*	j	*ee-loonga*	q	*koo*	x	*eeks*
d	*dee*	k	*kap-pa*	r	*air-ay*	y	*eepseelon*
e	*ay*	l	*el-lay*	s	*es-say*	z	*tsay-ta*
f	*ef-fay*	m	*em-may*	t	*tee*		
g	*jee*	n	*en-nay*	u	*oo*		

REPLIES YOU MAY BE GIVEN

Pronto
Hello

Sono io/All'apparecchio
Speaking

Con chi vuole parlare?
Who would you like to speak to?

Ha sbagliato numero
You've got the wrong number

Chi parla?
Who's calling?

Attenda in linea, prego
Hold the line, please

Mi dispiace, non c'è
I'm sorry, he/she's not in

Posso richiamarla?
Can I call you back?

Che numero ha?
What is your number?

Tornerà alle...
He/she'll be back at ... o'clock

Richiami domani, per favore
Please call again tomorrow

Gli dirò che ha chiamato
I'll tell him you called

THINGS YOU'LL SEE

apparecchio	phone
cabina telefonica	telephone box
centralino	local exchange, operator
chiamata	call
chiamata in teleselezione	direct dialling
chiamata interurbana	long-distance call
chiamata urbana	local call
comporre il numero	dial
fuori servizio	out of order
gettoni	telephone tokens
guida telefonica	telephone directory
il servizio è gratuito	free service
inserire le monete	insert coins
moneta	coin
numeri utili	useful numbers
numero	number
Pagine Gialle	Yellow Pages
prefissi telefonici	codes
riagganciare	hang up
ricevitore	receiver
scatto	unit
scheda telefonica	phonecard
selezionare il numero	dial the number
servizio guasti	faults service
sollevare	to lift
vigili del fuoco	fire brigade

EMERGENCIES

Information on local health services can be obtained from tourist information offices but in an emergency, dial 113, which is a general emergency number (like 999 in Britain). Dial 115 for the fire brigade and 118 for an ambulance.

Remember that there is more than one type of police force in Italy: **carabinieri** are a military force and **polizia** are a civil force dealing with crime. In case of emergency, dial either 113 for **polizia** or 112 for **carabinieri**.

For emergency breakdown services dial 116 (or 01 in the provinces of Potenza, Catanzaro, Lecce or Caltanisetta) and you will be put in contact with the **ACI** (Italian Automobile Club) who will provide immediate assistance. There is an agreement between **ACI** and foreign automobile associations, so that members of the British AA or RAC can turn to **ACI** in an emergency (see also MOTORING page 37).

USEFUL WORDS AND PHRASES

accident	l'incidente	*eencheedentay*
ambulance	l'ambulanza	*amboolantza*
assault	aggredire	*ag-gredeeray*
breakdown	il guasto	*gwasto*
break down	guastarsi	*gwastarsee*
burglar	il ladro	*ladro*
burglary	il furto	*foorto*
casualty department	il pronto soccorso	*pronto sok-korso*
crash *(noun)*	l'incidente	*eencheedentay*
(verb)	avere un incidente	*avairay oon eencheedentay*
emergency	l'emergenza	*emairjentza*
fire *(flames)*	il fuoco	*fwoko*
(event)	l'incendio	*eenchend-yo*
fire brigade	i vigili del fuoco	*veejeelee del fwoko*

flood	l'inondazione	*eenondatz-yonay*
injured	ferito	*faireeto*
lose	perdere	*pairdairay*
pickpocket	il borsaiolo	*borsi-olo*
police	la polizia	*poleetzee-a*
police station	il commissariato di polizia	*kom-mees-sar-yato dee poleetzee-a*
rob	derubare	*dairoobaray*
steal	rubare	*roobaray*
theft	il furto	*foorto*
thief	il ladro	*ladro*
tow	rimorchiare	*reemork-yaray*

Help!
Aiuto!
I-ooto

Look out!
(Stia) attento!
(stee-a) at-tento

Stop!
Si fermi!
see fairmee

This is an emergency!
Questa è un'emergenza!
kwesta eh oon emairjentza

Get an ambulance!
Chiami un'ambulanza!
k-yamee oon amboolantza

Hurry up!
Presto!
presto

Please send an ambulance to ...
Per favore, mandate un'ambulanza a...
pair favoray mandatay oon amboolantza a

Please come to ...
Venite, per favore, a...
veneetay pair favoray a

My address is ...
Il mio indirizzo è...
eel mee-o eendeereetzo eh

We've had a break-in
Ci sono entrati i ladri in casa
chee sono entratee ee ladree een kaza

There's a fire at ...
C'è un incendio a...
cheh oon eenchend-yo a

Someone's been injured
C'è un ferito
cheh oon faireeto

Someone's been knocked down
È stata investita una persona
eh stata eenvesteeta oona pairsona

He's passed out
È svenuto
eh svenooto

My passport/car has been stolen
Mi hanno rubato il passaporto/la macchina
mee an-no roobato eel pas-saporto/la mak-keena

I've lost my traveller's cheques
Ho perso i miei traveller's cheques
oh pairso ee mee-ay 'traveller's cheques'

I want to report a stolen credit card
Vorrei denunciare il furto di una carta di credito
vor-ray denooncharay eel foorto dee oona karta dee kraydeeto

It was stolen from my room
È stato rubato dalla mia camera
eh stato roobato dal-la mee-a kamaira

I lost it in the park/at the station
L'ho perso nel parco/alla stazione
lo pairso nel parko/al-la statz-yonay

My luggage has gone missing
I miei bagagli sono spariti
ee mee-ay bagal-yee sono spareetee

Has my luggage been found yet?
Sono stati ritrovati i miei bagagli?
sono statee reetrovatee ee mee-ay bagal-yee

I've crashed my car/had a crash
Ho avuto un incidente con la macchina
oh avooto oon eencheedentay kon la mak-keena

My car's been broken into
La mia macchina è stata forzata
la mee-a mak-keena eh stata fortzata

The registration number is ...
Il numero di targa è...
eel noomairo dee targa eh

I've been mugged *(said by a man)*
Sono stato aggredito
sono stato ag-gredeeto

(said by a woman)
Sono stata aggredita
sono stata ag-gredeeta

My son's missing
Mio figlio è scomparso
mee-o feel-yo eh skomparso

He has fair/brown hair
Ha i capelli biondi/castani
a ee kapel-lee b-yondee/kastanee

He's ... years old
Ha... anni
a ... an-nee

I've locked myself out *(said by a man)*
Sono rimasto chiuso fuori
sono reemasto k-yoozo fworee

(said by a woman)
Sono rimasta chiusa fuori
sono reemasta k-yooza fworee

He's drowning!
Sta annegando!
sta an-negando

He/she can't swim!
Non sa nuotare!
non sa nwotaray

THINGS YOU'LL SEE

carabinieri	police
commissariato di polizia	police station
emergenza sanitaria	ambulance
farmacia di turno	late-night chemist's
numeri di emergenza	emergency phone numbers
ospedale	hospital
polizia	police

→

polizia stradale	traffic police
pronto intervento	emergency service
pronto soccorso	first aid
soccorso alpino	mountain rescue
soccorso stradale	breakdown service
telefono	telephone
vigili del fuoco	fire brigade

THINGS YOU'LL HEAR

Il suo/vostro indirizzo, prego?
What's your address, please?

Dove si trova/vi trovate?
Where are you?

Può descriverlo?
Can you describe it/him?

HEALTH

Under EC Social Security regulations visitors from the UK qualify for free medical treatment on the same basis as the Italians themselves. If you want to make sure of being in possession of all necessary documentation, you should obtain a T4 from a main post office, fill in the attached E111 and get it stamped at the post office before travelling. With the E111, you'll also get a leaflet explaining how to obtain treatment. Once in Italy you can get information from the Local Health Unit, the **USL (Unità Sanitaria Locale)**.

If you should need medical treatment, hand your E111 to the **USL** and you will be given a certificate of entitlement. Ask to see a list of the scheme's doctors. You will be entitled to treatment from any of these, free of charge. For prescribed medicines a standard charge will be made at the chemist's (see also SHOPS AND SERVICES page 79). If you do not get the certificate from the Local Health Unit, you will have to pay for treatment and getting refunds later can be much more problematic. In any case the refund would only be partial. If a doctor thinks you need hospital treatment, he will give you a certificate (**proposta di ricovero**). This entitles you to free treatment in certain hospitals, a list of which will be available at the **USL**. If you cannot contact the **USL** office before going into hospital, show the E111 to the hospital authorities and ask them to get in touch with the **USL** about your right to free treatment.

If you need dental treatment in Italy, you should be prepared to pay. Most dentists are private and it could take months to get free treatment from the **USL**.

USEFUL WORDS AND PHRASES

accident	l'incidente	*eencheedentay*
ambulance	l'ambulanza	*amboolantza*
anaemic	anemico	*anaymeeko*
appendicitis	l'appendicite	*ap-pendeecheetay*
appendix	l'appendice	*ap-pendeechay*

aspirin	l'aspirina	*aspeereena*
asthma	l'asma	*azma*
backache	il mal di schiena	*mal dee sk-yayna*
bandage	la fascia, benda	*fasha, benda*
bite *(by dog, snake)*	il morso	*morso*
(by insect)	la puntura	*poontoora*
bladder	la vescica	*vesheeka*
blister	la vescica	*vesheeka*
blood	il sangue	*sangway*
blood donor	il donatore di sangue	*donatoray dee sangway*
burn	la bruciatura	*broo-chatoora*
cancer	il cancro	*kankro*
chemist	il farmacista	*farmacheesta*
chest	il petto	*pet-to*
chickenpox	la varicella	*vareechel-la*
cold	il raffreddore	*raf-fred-doray*
concussion	la commozione cerebrale	*kom-motz-yonay chairebralay*
constipation	la stitichezza	*steeteeketza*
contact lenses	le lenti a contatto	*lentee a kontat-to*
corn	il callo	*kal-lo*
cough	la tosse	*tos-say*
cut	il taglio	*tal-yo*
dentist	il dentista	*denteesta*
diabetes	il diabete	*dee-abaytay*
diarrhoea	la diarrea	*dee-aray-a*
doctor	il dottore, il medico	*dot-toray, medeeko*
earache	il mal d'orecchi	*mal dorek-kee*
fever	la febbre	*feb-bray*
filling	l'otturazione	*ot-tooratz-yonay*
first aid	il pronto soccorso	*pronto sok-korso*
flu	l'influenza	*eenfloo-entza*
fracture	la frattura	*frat-toora*
German measles	la rosolia	*rozolee-a*
haemorrhage	l'emorragia	*emor-rajee-a*
hayfever	il raffreddore da fieno	*raf-fred-doray da f-yeno*

headache	il mal di testa	*mal dee testa*
heart	il cuore	*kworay*
heart attack	l'infarto	*eenfarto*
hospital	l'ospedale	*ospedalay*
ill	malato	*malato*
indigestion	l'indigestione	*eendeejest-yonay*
injection	l'iniezione	*een-yetz-yonay*
itch	il prurito	*prooreeto*
kidney	il rene	*raynay*
lump	il nodulo	*nodoolo*
measles	il morbillo	*morbeel-lo*
migraine	l'emicrania	*emeekranee-a*
mumps	gli orecchioni	*orekk-yonee*
nausea	la nausea	*now-zay-a*
nurse	l'infermiera	*eenfairmee-aira*
(male)	l'infermiere	*eenfairmee-airay*
operation	l'operazione	*opairatz-yonay*
optician	l'ottico	*ot-teeko*
pain	il dolore	*doloray*
penicillin	la penicillina	*peneecheel-leena*
plaster	il cerotto	*chairot-to*
plaster of Paris	il gesso	*jes-so*
pneumonia	la polmonite	*polmoneetay*
pregnant	incinta	*eencheenta*
prescription	la ricetta	*reechet-ta*
rheumatism	il reumatismo	*ray-oomateezmo*
scald	la scottatura	*skot-tatoora*
scratch	il graffio	*graf-fee-o*
smallpox	il vaiolo	*vi-olo*
sore throat	il mal di gola	*mal dee gola*
splinter	la scheggia	*skej-ja*
sprain	la slogatura,	*zlogatura,*
	lo strappo muscolare	*strap-po mooskolaray*
sting	la puntura	*poontura*
stomach	lo stomaco	*stomako*
temperature	la febbre	*feb-bray*
tonsils	le tonsille	*tonseel-lay*

toothache	il mal di denti	*mal dee dentee*
travel sickness	il mal d'auto	*mal dowto*
ulcer	l'ulcera	*oolchaira*
vaccination	la vaccinazione	*vacheenatz-yonay*
vomit	vomitare	*vomeetaray*
whooping cough	la pertosse	*pairtos-say*

I have a pain in …
Mi fa male…
mee fa malay

I do not feel well
Non mi sento bene
non mee sento baynay

I feel faint
Mi sento svenire
mee sento zveneeray

I feel sick
Ho la nausea
oh la now-zay-a

I feel dizzy
Mi gira la testa
mee jeera la testa

It hurts here
Mi fa male qui
mee fa malay kwee

It's a sharp/dull pain
È un dolore acuto/sordo
eh oon doloray akooto/sordo

It hurts all the time
Mi fa continuamente male
mee fa konteenoo-amentay malay

It only hurts now and then
Non mi fa sempre male
non mee fa sempray malay

It hurts when you touch it
Mi fa male quando lo tocca
mee fa malay kwando lo tok-ka

It hurts more at night
Mi fa male di più di notte
mee fa malay dee p-yoo dee not-tay

It stings
Brucia
broocha

It aches
Fa male
fa malay

I have a temperature
Ho la febbre
oh la feb-bray

I need a prescription for ...
Avrei bisogno di una ricetta per...
avray beezon-yo dee oona reechet-ta pair

I normally take ...
Generalmente prendo...
jenairalmentay prendo

I'm allergic to ... *(said by a man/woman)*
Sono allergico/allergica a...
sono al-lairjeeko/al-lairjeeka a

Have you got anything for ...?
Ha qualcosa per...?
a kwalkoza pair

117

Do I need a prescription for ...?
C'è bisogno della ricetta per...?
cheh beezon-yo del-la reechet-ta pair

I have lost a filling
Ho perso un'otturazione
oh pairso oon ot-tooratz-yonay

Will he/she be all right?
Starà bene?
stara baynay

Will he/she need an operation?
Dovrà essere operato/operata?
dovra essairay operato/operata

How is he/she?
Come sta?
komay sta

THINGS YOU'LL SEE

ambulanza	ambulance
anticamera	waiting room
autoambulanza	ambulance
chirurgia	surgery
chirurgo	surgeon
degente	in-patient
dermatologo	dermatologist
dottore	doctor
farmacia di turno	duty chemist's, late-night chemist's
ginecologo	gynaecologist
infermeria	infirmary
medico di turno	doctor on duty
oculista	oculist
orario di visita	visiting hours

→

ospedale	hospital
otorinolaringoiatra	ear, nose and throat specialist
ottico	optician
pronto soccorso	first aid, casualty ward
reparto	ward
sala operatoria	operating theatre
specialista	specialist

THINGS YOU'LL HEAR

Da inghiottire con acqua
With water

Da masticare
Chew them

Una/due/tre volte al giorno
Once/twice/three times a day

Prima di andare a letto
At bedtime

Al mattino
In the morning

Cosa prende normalmente?
What do you normally take?

Penso che lei debba andare dal medico
I think you should see a doctor

Mi dispiace, non ne abbiamo/vendiamo
I'm sorry, we don't have/sell that

Per questo c'è bisogno della ricetta
You need a prescription for that

CONVERSION TABLES

DISTANCES

A mile is 1.6km. To convert kilometres to miles, divide the km by 8 and multiply by 5. Convert miles to km by dividing the miles by 5 and multiplying by 8.

miles	0.62	1.24	1.86	2.43	3.11	3.73	4.35	6.21
miles or km	**1**	**2**	**3**	**4**	**5**	**6**	**7**	**10**
km	1.61	3.22	4.83	6.44	8.05	9.66	11.27	16.10

WEIGHTS

The kilogram is equivalent to 2lb 3oz. To convert kg to lbs, divide by 5 and multiply by 11. One ounce is about 28 grams, and eight ounces about 227 grams; 1lb is therefore about 454 grams.

lbs	2.20	4.41	6.61	8.82	11.02	13.23	19.84	22.04
lbs or kg	**1**	**2**	**3**	**4**	**5**	**6**	**9**	**10**
kg	0.45	0.91	1.36	1.81	2.27	2.72	4.08	4.53

TEMPERATURE

To convert Celsius degrees into Fahrenheit, the accurate method is to multiply the °C figure by 1.8 and add 32. Similarly, to convert °F to °C, subtract 32 from the °F figure and divide by 1.8.

°C	-10	0	5	10	20	30	36.9	40	100
°F	14	32	41	50	68	77	98.4	104	212

LIQUIDS

A litre is about 1.75 pints; a gallon is roughly 4.5 litres.

gals	0.22	0.44	1.10	2.20	4.40	6.60	11.00
gals or litres	**1**	**2**	**5**	**10**	**20**	**30**	**50**
litres	4.54	9.10	22.73	45.46	90.92	136.40	227.30

TYRE PRESSURES

lb/sq in	18	20	22	24	26	28	30	33
kg/sq cm	1.3	1.4	1.5	1.7	1.8	2.0	2.1	2.3

MINI-DICTIONARY

a un/uno/una/un' *(see page 5)*
about: about 16 circa 16
  a book about Venice un libro su
  Venezia
accelerator l'acceleratore
accident l'incidente
accommodation l'alloggio, il posto
ache il dolore
adaptor il riduttore
address l'indirizzo
adhesive l'adesivo
after dopo
afternoon il pomeriggio
aftershave il dopobarba
again di nuovo
against contro
Aids l'Aids
air l'aria
air-conditioning l'aria
  condizionata
aircraft l'aereo
airline la linea aerea
airport l'aeroporto
airport bus l'autobus navetta
alarm clock la sveglia
alcohol l'alcol
all tutto
  all the streets tutte le strade
  that's all questo è tutto
almost quasi
alone solo
Alps le Alpi
already già
always sempre
am: I am (io) sono
ambulance l'ambulanza
America l'America
American *(man)* l'americano
  (woman) l'americana

(adj) americano
and e
ankle la caviglia
anorak la giacca a vento
another un altro, un'altra
anti-freeze l'antigelo
antique shop il negozio di
  antiquariato
antiseptic l'antisettico
apartment l'appartamento
aperitif l'aperitivo
appetite l'appetito
apple la mela
application form il modulo per la
  domanda
appointment l'appuntamento
apricot l'albicocca
are: you are (Lei) è
  (singular, familiar) (tu) sei
  (plural) (voi) siete
  we are (noi) siamo
  they are (loro) sono
arm il braccio
arrive arrivare
art l'arte
art gallery la galleria d'arte
artist l'artista
as: as soon as possible (il) più
  presto possibile
ashtray il portacenere
asleep: he's asleep dorme
aspirin l'aspirina
at: at the post office all'ufficio
  postale
  at night di notte
  at 3 o'clock alle tre
attractive attraente
aunt la zia
Australia l'Australia

Australian *(man)* l'australiano
  (woman) l'australiana
  (adj) australiano
automatic automatico
away: is it far away? è lontano?
  go away! vattene!
awful terribile, orribile
axe l'ascia
axle il semiasse

baby il bambino
  (female) la bambina
back *(not front)* la parte posteriore
  (body) la schiena
  to come back tornare
bacon la pancetta
  bacon and eggs uova e pancetta
bad cattivo
bag la borsa
baggage claim il ritiro bagagli
bait l'esca
bake cuocere (al forno)
baker's la panetteria
balcony il balcone
ball *(football etc)* la palla
  (tennis etc) la pallina
banana la banana
band *(musicians)* la banda
bandage la fascia
bank la banca
banknote la banconota
bar *(drinks)* il bar
  bar of chocolate la tavoletta di
  cioccolata
barbecue il barbecue
  (occasion) la grigliata all'aperto
barber's il barbiere
bargain l'affare
basement il seminterrato
basin *(sink)* il lavabo
basket il cestino
  (in supermarket) il cestello
bath il bagno
  (tub) la vasca da bagno

to have a bath fare il bagno
bathroom il bagno
battery la batteria
beach la spiaggia
beans i fagioli
beard la barba
beautiful bello
because perché
bed il letto
bed linen le lenzuola
bedroom la camera da letto
beef il manzo
beer la birra
before ... prima di...
beginner il/la principiante
behind dietro
  behind ... dietro a...
beige beige
bell *(church)* la campana
  (door) il campanello
below sotto
belt la cintura
  (technical) la cinghia
beside ... vicino a...
best il migliore
better (than) migliore (di)
between ... fra...
bicycle la bicicletta
big grande
bikini il bikini
bill il conto
bin liner il sacchetto per la
  pattumiera
bird l'uccello
Biro ® la penna a sfera
birthday il compleanno
  happy birthday! buon
  compleanno!
biscuit il biscotto
bite *(noun: by dog)* il morso
  (by insect) la puntura
  (verb: by dog) mordere
  (by insect) pungere
bitter amaro

black nero
blackberry la mora
blackcurrant il ribes nero
blanket la coperta
bleach la varechina
(verb: hair) ossigenare
blind *(cannot see)* cieco
(on window) la tenda avvolgibile
blizzard la bufera di neve
blond(e) *(adj)* biondo
blood il sangue
blouse la camicetta
blue azzurro
(darker) blu
boat la nave
(small) la barca
(passenger) il battello
body il corpo
boil *(verb: of water)* bollire
(egg etc) far bollire
bolt *(noun: on door)* il catenaccio
(verb) chiudere con il catenaccio
bone l'osso
(fish) la lisca
bonnet *(car)* il cofano
book *(noun)* il libro
(verb) prenotare
booking office la biglietteria
bookshop la libreria
boot *(car)* il portabagagli
(footwear) lo stivale
border il confine
boring noioso
born: I was born in London sono
nato a Londra
I was born in 1965 sono nato nel
1965
both: both of them tutti e due
both ... and ... sia... che...
bottle la bottiglia
bottle-opener l'apribottiglie
bottom il fondo
(part of body) il sedere
at the bottom (of) in fondo (a)

bowl la scodella
(mixing bowl) la terrina
box la scatola
(of wood etc) la cassetta
box office il botteghino
boy il ragazzo
boyfriend il ragazzo
bra il reggiseno
bracelet il braccialetto
braces le bretelle
brake *(noun)* il freno
(verb) frenare
brandy il brandy
bread il pane
breakdown *(car)* il guasto
(nervous) l'esaurimento nervoso
I've had a breakdown *(car)* ho
avuto un guasto
breakfast la colazione
breathe respirare
bridge il ponte
the Bridge of Sighs il Ponte dei
Sospiri
briefcase la cartella
British britannico
brochure l'opuscolo
broken rotto
broken leg la gamba rotta
brooch la spilla
brother il fratello
brown marrone
bruise il livido
brush *(noun: hair)* la spazzola
(paint) il pennello
(cleaning) la scopa
(verb: hair) spazzolare
bucket il secchio
building l'edificio
bumper il paraurti
burglar il ladro
burn *(noun)* la bruciatura
(verb) bruciare
bus l'autobus, la corriera
business l'affare

123

it's none of your business non sono affari tuoi
bus station la stazione degli autobus
busy *(occupied)* occupato
(bar) animato
but ma
butcher's la macelleria
butter il burro
button il bottone
buy comprare
by: by the window vicino alla finestra
by Friday entro venerdì
by myself da solo
written by ... scritto da...

cabbage il cavolo
cable car la funivia
café il caffè, il bar
cagoule il K-way ®
cake la torta
cake shop la pasticceria
calculator il calcolatore
call: what's it called? come si chiama?
camcorder la videocamera
camera la macchina fotografica
campsite il campeggio
camshaft l'albero a camme
can *(tin)* la lattina
can: can I have ...? posso avere...?
can you ...? potreste...?
he/she can't ... non può...
Canada il Canada
Canadian *(man)* il canadese
(woman) la canadese
(adj) canadese
canal il canale
candle la candela
canoe la canoa
cap *(bottle)* il tappo
(hat) il berretto
car l'auto, la macchina

caravan la roulotte
carburettor il carburatore
card *(for birthday etc)* il biglietto
playing cards le carte da gioco
cardigan il cardigan
careful attento
be careful! stia attento!
caretaker il portinaio
(female) la portinaia
carpet il tappeto
carrot la carota
carry-cot il porte-enfant
case *(suitcase)* la valigia
cash *(noun)* il denaro
(verb) riscuotere
to pay cash pagare in contanti
cash dispenser lo sportello automatico
cassette la cassetta
cassette player il mangianastri
castle il castello
cat il gatto
cathedral la cattedrale
Catholic cattolico
cauliflower il cavolfiore
cave la grotta
cemetery il cimitero
central heating il riscaldamento centrale
centre il centro
certificate il certificato
chair la sedia
change *(noun: money)* il cambio
(verb: money, trains) cambiare
(clothes) cambiarsi
cheap economico, a buon mercato
check-in il check-in
check in fare il check-in
cheers! *(toast)* alla salute!, cin cin!
cheese il formaggio
chemist's la farmacia
cheque l'assegno
cheque book il libretto degli assegni
cheque card la carta assegni

cherry la ciliegia
chess gli scacchi
chest *(part of body)* il petto
   (furniture) il baule
chest of drawers il cassettone
chewing gum il chewing-gum
chicken il pollo
child il bambino
   (female) la bambina
children i bambini
china la porcellana
chips la patatine fritte
chocolate la cioccolata
   box of chocolates una scatola di
   cioccolatini
chop *(food)* la costoletta
   (verb: cut) tagliare (a pezzetti)
Christian name il nome di
   battesimo
church la chiesa
cigar il sigaro
cigarette la sigaretta
cinema il cinema
city la città
city centre il centro (della città)
class la classe
classical music la musica classica
clean *(adj)* pulito
clear *(obvious)* chiaro
   (water) limpido
clever bravo, intelligente
cling film la pellicola adesiva
clock l'orologio
close *(near)* vicino (a)
   (stuffy) soffocante
   (verb) chiudere
closed chiuso
clothes i vestiti
clubs *(cards)* fiori
clutch la frizione
coach la corriera
   (of train) la carrozza
coach station la stazione delle
   corriere

coat il capotto
coathanger l'attaccapanni
cockroach lo scarafaggio
coffee il caffè
coin la moneta
cold *(illness)* il raffreddore
   (adj) freddo
   I have a cold ho un raffreddore
Coliseum il Colosseo
collar il colletto
collection *(stamps etc)* la collezione
   (postal) la levata
colour il colore
colour film la pellicola a colori
comb *(noun)* il pettine
   (verb) pettinare
come venire
   I come from ... sono di...
   we came last week siamo arrivati
   la settimana scorsa
   come here! vieni qui!
Common Market il Mercato
   Comune
compact disc il compact disc
compartment lo scompartimento
complicated complicato
computer il computer
concert il concerto
conditioner *(hair)* il balsamo
condom il preservativo
conductor *(bus)* il bigliettaio
   (orchestra) il direttore
congratulations! congratulazioni!
consulate il consolato
contact lenses le lenti a contatto
contraceptive il contraccettivo
cook *(noun)* il cuoco
   (female) la cuoca
   (verb) cucinare
cooker il fornello
cooking utensils gli utensili da
   cucina
cool fresco
cork il tappo

125

corkscrew il cavatappi
corner l'angolo
corridor il corridoio
cosmetics i cosmetici
cost *(verb)* costare
  what does it cost? quanto costa?
cotton il cotone
cotton wool il cotone idrofilo
cough *(noun)* la tosse
  (verb) tossire
country *(state)* il paese
  (not town) la campagna
cousin il cugino
  (female) la cugina
crab il granchio
cramp il crampo
crayfish il gambero
cream *(for cake etc)* la crema, la panna
  (lotion) la crema
credit card la carta di credito
crew l'equipaggio
crisps le patatine
crowded affollato
cruise la crociera
crutches le stampelle
cry *(verb: weep)* piangere
  (shout) gridare
cucumber il cetriolo
cufflinks i gemelli
cup la tazza
cupboard l'armadio
curlers i bigodini
curls i ricci
curry il curry
curtain la tenda
customs la dogana
cut *(noun)* il taglio
  (verb) tagliare

dad il papà, il babbo
damp umido
dance *(noun)* il ballo
  (verb) ballare

dangerous pericoloso
dark scuro
daughter la figlia
day il giorno
dead morto
deaf sordo
dear caro
deckchair la sedia a sdraio
deep profondo
delayed in ritardo
deliberately deliberatamente
dentist il/la dentista
dentures la dentiera
deodorant il deodorante
department store il grande magazzino
departure la partenza
departure lounge la sala d'attesa
develop *(film)* sviluppare
diamond *(jewel)* il diamante
diamonds *(cards)* quadri
diary il diario
dictionary il dizionario
die morire
diesel il diesel
different diverso
  that's different! è diverso!
  I'd like a different one ne vorrei un altro
difficult difficile
dining room la sala da pranzo
dinner la cena
directory *(telephone)* la guida telefonica
dirty sporco
disabled invalido
disposable nappies i pannolini usa e getta
distributor *(in car)* il distributore
dive *(noun)* il tuffo
  (verb) tuffarsi
diving board il trampolino
divorced divorziato
do fare

how do you do? piacere di conoscerla

doctor il dottore
(female) la dottoressa

document il documento

dog il cane

doll la bambola

dollar il dollaro

door la porta

double room la camera doppia

doughnut il krapfen

down giù

drawing pin la puntina da disegno

dress il vestito

drink *(noun)* la bibita
(verb) bere

would you like a drink? vorresti qualcosa da bere?

drinking water l'acqua potabile

drive *(verb)* guidare

driver il guidatore
(female) la guidatrice
(of bus, lorry etc) l'autista

driving licence la patente di guida

drunk ubriaco

dry asciutto
(wine) secco

dry-cleaner's la lavanderia a secco

dummy *(for baby)* la tettarella

during durante

dustbin la pattumiera

duster lo straccio per la polvere

duty-free il duty free

duvet il piumino

each *(every)* ogni
a thousand lire each mille lire ciascuno

ear l'orecchio
ears le orecchie

early presto

earrings gli orecchini

east l'est

easy facile

eat mangiare

EC la CEE

egg l'uovo

either: either of them l'uno o l'altro
either ... or ... o... o...

elastic elastico

elastic band l'elastico

elbow il gomito

electric elettrico

electricity l'elettricità

else: something else qualcos'altro
someone else qualcun'altro
somewhere else da qualche altra parte

embarrassing imbarazzante

embassy l'ambasciata

embroidery il ricamo

emergency l'emergenza

emergency brake il freno d'emergenza

emergency exit l'uscita di sicurezza

empty vuoto

end la fine

engaged *(couple)* fidanzato
(occupied) occupato

engine *(motor)* il motore
(railway) la locomotiva

England l'Inghilterra

English inglese

Englishman l'inglese

Englishwoman l'inglese

enlargement l'ampliamento

enough abbastanza

entrance l'entrata

envelope la busta

escalator la scala mobile

especially particolarmente

estate agent l'agente immobiliare

evening la sera

every ogni

everyone ognuno, tutti

everything tutto

everywhere dappertutto

example l'esempio

for example per esempio
excellent ottimo, eccellente
excess baggage il bagaglio in eccesso
exchange *(verb)* scambiare
exchange rate il tasso di cambio
excursion l'escursione
excuse me! *(to get past)* permesso!
(to get attention) mi scusi!
(when sneezing etc) scusate!
exit l'uscita
expensive caro, costoso
extension lead la prolunga
eye l'occhio
eyes gli occhi

face la faccia
faint *(unclear)* indistinto
(verb) svenire
fair *(funfair)* il luna park
(trade) la fiera
it's not fair non è giusto
false teeth la dentiera
family la famiglia
fan *(ventilator)* il ventilatore
(enthusiast) l'ammiratore
fan belt la cinghia della ventola
fantastic fantastico
far lontano
how far is it to ...? quanto dista da qui...?
fare la tariffa
farm la fattoria
farmer l'agricoltore
fashion la moda
fast veloce
fat *(person)* grasso
(on meat etc) il grasso
father il padre
fax *(noun)* il fax
(verb: document) spedire via fax
feel *(touch)* tastare
I feel hot ho caldo
I feel like ... ho voglia di...

I don't feel well non mi sento bene
felt-tip pen il pennarello
fence lo steccato
ferry il traghetto
fever la febbre
fiancé il fidanzato
fiancée la fidanzata
field il campo
filling *(in tooth)* l'otturazione
(in sandwich, cake etc) il ripieno
film *(for camera)* la pellicola
(at cinema) il film
filter il filtro
finger il dito
fire il fuoco
(blaze) l'incendio
fire extinguisher l'estintore
fireworks i fuochi d'artificio
first primo
first aid il pronto soccorso
first floor il primo piano
fish il pesce
fishing la pesca
to go fishing andare a pesca
fishmonger's il pescivendolo
fizzy frizzante
flag la bandiera
flash *(camera)* il flash
flat *(apartment)* l'appartamento
(level) piatto
flavour il gusto
flea la pulce
flight il volo
flip-flops gli infradito
flippers le pinne
floor *(storey)* il piano
(ground) il pavimento
flour la farina
Florence Firenze
flower il fiore
flute il flauto
fly *(insect)* la mosca
(verb) volare

I'm flying to London sto
andando a Londra in aereo
fog la nebbia
folk music la musica folk
food il cibo
food poisoning l'intossicazione
alimentare
foot il piede
football *(game)* il calcio
(ball) il pallone
for per
for me per me
what for? per che cosa?
foreigner lo straniero
forest la foresta
forget dimenticare
fork *(for food)* la forchetta
fortnight due settimane
fountain pen la penna stilografica
fourth quarto
France la Francia
free *(not engaged)* libero
(no charge) gratis
freezer il congelatore
French francese
Frenchman il francese
Frenchwoman la francese
fridge il frigorifero
friend l'amico
(female) l'amica
friendly cordiale
fringe *(hair)* la frangia
front: in front of you davanti a te
frost il gelo
fruit la frutta
fruit juice il succo di frutta
fry friggere
frying pan la padella
full pieno
I'm full (up) sono sazio
full board la pensione completa
funny divertente
(odd) strano
furniture i mobili

garage il garage
garden il giardino
garlic l'aglio
gas-permeable lenses le lenti semi-
rigide
gate il cancello
(at airport) l'uscita
gay *(homosexual)* omosessuale, gay
gear *(car)* il cambio
gear lever la leva del cambio
gel *(hair)* il gel
Genoa Genova
gents *(toilet)* la toilette degli uomini
German *(man)* il tedesco
(woman) la tedesca
(adj) tedesco
Germany la Germania
get *(obtain)* ricevere
(fetch: person) chiamare
(something) prendere
have you got ...? ha...?
to get the train prendere il treno
get back: we get back tomorrow
torniamo domani
to get something back riavere
indietro qualcosa
get in entrare
(arrive) arrivare
get off *(bus etc)* scendere (da)
get on *(bus etc)* salire (su)
get out uscire (da)
get up alzarsi
gift il regalo
gin il gin
ginger *(spice)* lo zenzero
girl la ragazza
girlfriend la ragazza
give dare
glad contento
glass *(material)* il vetro
(for drinking) il bicchiere
glasses gli occhiali
gloss prints le fotografie su carta
lucida

gloves i guanti
glue la colla
go andare
  (depart) partire
gold l'oro
good buono
  good! bene!
goodbye arrivederci
government il governo
granddaughter la nipote
grandfather il nonno
grandmother la nonna
grandparents i nonni
grandson il nipote
grapes l'uva
grass l'erba
Great Britain la Gran Bretagna
Greece la Grecia
Greek *(man)* il greco
  (woman) la greca
  (adj) greco
green verde
grey grigio
grill la griglia
grocer's il negozio di alimentari
ground floor il pianterreno
groundsheet il telone
  impermeabile
guarantee *(noun)* la garanzia
  (verb) garantire
guard la guardia
guide *(person)* la guida
guide book la guida
guitar la chitarra
gun *(rifle)* il fucile
  (pistol) la pistola

hair i capelli
haircut il taglio
hairdresser's il parrucchiere
hair dryer l'asciugacapelli
hair spray la lacca per i capelli
half metà
  half an hour mezz'ora

half board mezza pensione
ham il prosciutto
hamburger l'hamburger
hammer il martello
hand la mano
handbag la borsetta
handbrake il freno a mano
handkerchief il fazzoletto
handle *(door)* la maniglia
handsome bello, attraente
hangover i postumi della sbornia
happy felice
harbour il porto
hard duro
  (difficult) difficile
hard lenses le lenti rigide
hardware shop il negozio di
  ferramenta
hat il cappello
have avere
  I don't have ... non ho...
  have you got ...? ha...?
  I have to go now devo andare
  adesso
he lui
head la testa
headache il mal di testa
headlights i fari
hear udire, sentire
hearing aid l'apparecchio acustico
heart il cuore
hearts *(cards)* cuori
heater il termosifone
heating il riscaldamento
heavy pesante
heel *(of foot)* il tallone
  (of shoe) il tacco
hello ciao
  (on phone) pronto
help *(noun)* l'aiuto
  (verb) aiutare
her: it's her è lei
  it's for her è per lei
  give it to her daglielo

her book il suo libro
her house la sua casa
her shoes le sue scarpe
her dresses i suoi vestiti
it's hers è suo
hi! salve!
high alto
highway code il codice della strada
hill la collina
him: it's him è lui
  it's for him è per lui
  give it to him daglielo
hire *(car, bike)* noleggiare
his: his book il suo libro
  his house la sua casa
  his shoes le sue scarpe
  his socks i suoi calzini
  it's his è suo
history la storia
hitchhike fare l'autostop
hobby il passatempo
holiday la vacanza
home: at home a casa
honest onesto
honey il miele
honeymoon la luna di miele
horn *(car)* il clacson
  (animal) il corno
horrible orribile
hospital l'ospedale
hour l'ora
house la casa
how? come?
hungry: I'm hungry ho fame
hurry: I'm in a hurry ho fretta
husband il marito

I io
ice il ghiaccio
ice cream il gelato
ice lolly il ghiacciolo
ice skates i pattini da ghiaccio
if se
ignition l'accensione

ill malato
immediately immediatamente
impossible impossibile
in: in English in inglese
  in the hotel nell'albergo
  in Venice a Venezia
indicator l'indicatore di direzione
indigestion l'indigestione
infection l'infezione
information le informazioni
injection l'iniezione
injury la ferita
ink l'inchiostro
inner tube la camera d'aria
insect l'insetto
insect repellent l'insettifugo
insomnia l'insonnia
instant coffee il caffè solubile
insurance l'assicurazione
interesting interessante
interpret interpretare
interpreter l'interprete
invitation l'invito
Ireland l'Irlanda
Irish irlandese
Irishman l'irlandese
Irishwoman l'irlandese
iron *(material)* il ferro
  (for clothes) il ferro da stiro
  (verb) stirare
is: he/she/it is ... (lui/lei/esso) è...
island l'isola
it esso
Italian *(man)* l'italiano
  (woman) l'italiana
  (adj) italiano
  the Italians gli italiani
Italy Italia
its suo

jacket la giacca
jam la marmellata
jazz il jazz
jeans i jeans

131

jellyfish la medusa
jeweller il gioielliere
job il lavoro
jog *(verb)* fare jogging
  to go for a jog andare a fare jogging
jogging il jogging
joke lo scherzo
journey il viaggio
jumper il maglione
just *(only)* solo
  it's just arrived è appena arrivato

kettle il bollitore
key la chiave
kidney il rene
kilo il chilo
kilometre il chilometro
kitchen la cucina
knee il ginocchio
knife il coltello
knit lavorare a maglia
knitwear la maglieria
know sapere
  (person) conoscere
  I don't know non so

label l'etichetta
lace il pizzo
laces *(of shoe)* i lacci
ladies *(toilet)* la toilette delle donne
lady la signora
lake il lago
lamb l'agnello
lamp la lampada
lampshade il paralume
land *(noun)* la terra
  (verb) atterrare
language la lingua
large grande
last *(final)* ultimo
  last week la settimana scorsa
  at last! finalmente!

late: it's getting late si sta facendo tardi
  the bus is late l'autobus è in ritardo
later più tardi
laugh ridere
laundry *(place)* la lavanderia
  (dirty clothes) la biancheria
laxative il lassativo
lazy pigro
leaf la foglia
leaflet il volantino
learn imparare
leather la pelle, il cuoio
left *(not right)* sinistra
  there's nothing left non c'è rimasto più nulla
left-luggage locker il desposito bagagli
leg la gamba
lemon il limone
lemonade la limonata
length la lunghezza
lens la lente
less meno
lesson la lezione
letter la lettera
letter box la cassetta delle lettere
lettuce la lattuga
library la biblioteca
licence la patente
life la vita
lift *(in building)* l'ascensore
  could you give me a lift? può darmi un passaggio?
light *(noun)* la luce
  (adj: not heavy) leggero
  (not dark) chiaro
light bulb la lampadina
light meter l'esposimetro
lighter l'accendino
lighter fuel il gas per accendini
like: I like you mi piaci
  I like swimming mi piace nuotare

it's like ... assomiglia a...
  like this one come questo
lime *(fruit)* il lime
lip salve il burro di cacao
lipstick il rossetto
liqueur il liquore
list l'elenco
litre il litro
litter i rifiuti
little *(small)* piccolo
  it's a little big è un po' grande
  just a little solo un po'
liver il fegato
lobster l'aragosta
lollipop il lecca lecca
long lungo
  how long does it take? quanto ci vuole?
long-distance *(call)* interurbano
lorry il camion
lost property office l'ufficio oggetti smarriti
lot: a lot molto
loud forte
  (colour) chiassoso
love *(verb)* amare
lover l'amante
low basso
luck la fortuna
  good luck! buona fortuna!
luggage i bagagli
luggage rack la reticella (per i bagagli)
lunch il pranzo

mad pazzo
magazine la rivista
mail la posta
make fare
make-up il trucco
man l'uomo
manager il direttore
manageress la direttrice
many: not many non molti

map la carta (geografica)
  a map of Rome una piantina di Roma
marble il marmo
margarine la margarina
market il mercato
marmalade la marmellata d'arance
married sposato
mascara il mascara
mass *(church)* la messa
mast l'albero
match *(light)* il fiammifero
  (sport) l'incontro
material *(cloth)* la stoffa
matter: it doesn't matter non importa
mattress il materasso
maybe forse
me: it's me sono io
  it's for me è per me
  give it to me dammelo
meal il pasto
mean: what does this mean? che cosa significa?
meat la carne
mechanic il meccanico
medicine la medicina
Mediterranean il Mediterraneo
meeting l'incontro
melon il melone
menu il menù
message il messaggio
midday mezzogiorno
middle: in the middle of the square in mezzo alla piazza
  in the middle of the night nel cuore della notte
midnight mezzanotte
Milan Milano
milk il latte
mine: it's mine è mio
mineral water l'acqua minerale
minute il minuto
mirror lo specchio

Miss Signorina
mistake l'errore
money i soldi
month il mese
monument il monumento
moon la luna
moped il motorino
more: more than ... più di...
  I want some more ne voglio
  ancora
morning la mattina
  in the morning di mattina
mosaic il mosaico
mosquito la zanzara
mother la madre
motorbike la motocicletta
motorboat il motoscafo
motorway l'autostrada
mountain la montagna
mountain bike la mountain bike
mouse il topo
mousse *(for hair)* la schiuma
moustache i baffi
mouth la bocca
move *(verb)* muovere
  (move house) traslocare
  don't move! non muoverti!
Mr Signor
Mrs Signora
much: much better molto meglio
  much slower molto più
  lentamente
  not much non molto
mug il tazzone
mum mamma
museum il museo
mushroom il fungo
music la musica
musical instrument lo strumento
  musicale
musician il musicista
mussels le cozze
must: I must devo
mustard la senape

my: my book il mio libro
  my bag la mia borsa
  my keys le mie chiavi
  my dresses i miei vestiti

nail *(metal)* il chiodo
  (finger) l'unghia
nail clippers il tagliaunghie
nail file la limetta per le unghie
nail polish lo smalto per le unghie
name il nome
  what's your name? come ti
  chiami?
Naples Napoli
nappy il pannolino
narrow stretto
near: near the door vicino alla
  porta
necessary necessario
neck il collo
necklace la collana
need: I need ... ho bisogno di...
  there's no need non c'è bisogno
needle l'ago
negative *(photo)* la negativa
neither: neither of them nè l'uno
  nè l'altro
  neither ... nor ... nè... nè...
nephew il nipote
never mai
  I never smoke non fumo mai
new nuovo
news le notizie
  (on radio) il notiziario
newsagent il giornalaio
newspaper il giornale
New Zealand la Nuova Zelanda
New Zealander *(man)* il
  neozelandese
  (woman) la neozelandese
  (adj) neozelandese
next prossimo
  next week la settimana prossima
  what next? e poi?

who's next? a chi tocca?
nice *(attractive)* carino, bello
  (pleasant) simpatico
  (to eat) buono
niece la nipote
night la notte
nightclub il night
nightdress la camicia da notte
night porter il portiere di notte
no *(response)* no
  I have no money non ho soldi
nobody nessuno
noisy rumoroso
north il nord
Northern Ireland l'Irlanda del
  Nord
nose il naso
not non
  he's not ... non è...
notebook il taccuino
nothing niente
novel il romanzo
now ora, adesso
nowhere da nessuna parte
nudist il/la nudista
number il numero
number plate la targa
nursery slope la discesa per
  principianti
nut la noce, la nocciola
  (for bolt) il dado

oars i remi
occasionally ogni tanto
octopus la piovra
of di
office l'ufficio
often spesso
oil l'olio
ointment l'unguento
OK OK
old vecchio
  how old are you? quanti anni
  hai?

olive l'oliva
olive oil l'olio d'oliva
omelette l'omelette
on su
  on the table sul tavolo
  a book on Venice un libro su
  Venezia
  on Monday di lunedì
one uno
onion la cipolla
only solo
open *(adj)* aperto
  (verb) aprire
operation l'operazione
operator l'operatore
  (female) l'operatrice
opposite: opposite the hotel di
  fronte all'albergo
optician l'ottico
or o
orange *(fruit)* l'arancia
  (colour) arancione
orange juice il succo d'arancia
orchestra l'orchestra
ordinary normale
organ *(music)* l'organo
other: the other (one) l'altro
our: our hotel il nostro albergo
  our car la nostra macchina
  it's ours è nostro
out: he's out è uscito
outside fuori
oven il forno
over *(above)* su, sopra
  over 100 più di cento
  over the river al di là del fiume
  it's over *(finished)* è finito
  over there laggiù
overtake sorpassare
oyster l'ostrica

pack of cards il mazzo di carte
package *(parcel)* il pacco
packet il pacchetto

padlock il lucchetto
Padua Padova
page la pagina
pain il dolore
paint la vernice
pair il paio
palace il palazzo
pale pallido
pancakes le frittelle
paper la carta
  (newspaper) il giornale
paracetamol la cibalgina ®
paraffin la paraffina
parcel il pacchetto
pardon? prego?
parents i genitori
park *(noun)* il parco
  (verb) parcheggiare
parsley il prezzemolo
parting *(hair)* la riga
party *(celebration)* la festa
  (group) il gruppo
  (political) il partito
passenger il passeggero
  (female) la passeggera
passport il passaporto
pasta la pasta
path il sentiero
pavement il marciapiede
pay pagare
peach la pesca
peanuts le arachidi
pear la pera
pearl la perla
peas i piselli
pedestrian il pedone
peg *(clothes)* la molletta
  (tent) il picchetto
pen la penna
pencil la matita
pencil sharpener il temperamatite
penfriend il/la corrispondente
penknife il temperino
people la gente

pepper il pepe
  (red, green) il peperone
peppermint la menta piperita
per: per person a persona
  per annum all'anno
perfect perfetto
perfume il profumo
perhaps forse
perm la permanente
petrol la benzina
petrol station la stazione di servizio
photograph *(noun)* la fotografia
  (verb) fotografare
photographer il fotografo
phrase book il vocabolarietto
piano il pianoforte
pickpocket il borsaiolo
picnic il picnic
piece il pezzo
pillow il cuscino
pin lo spillo
pineapple l'ananas
pink rosa
pipe *(for smoking)* la pipa
  (for water) il tubo
piston il pistone
pizza la pizza
place il posto
  at your place a casa tua
plant la pianta
plaster *(for cut)* il cerotto
plastic la plastica
plastic bag il sacchetto di plastica
plate il piatto
platform il binario
play *(theatre)* la commedia
  (verb) giocare
please per favore
plug *(electrical)* la spina
  (sink) il tappo
pocket la tasca
poison il veleno
police la polizia
policeman il poliziotto

police station la stazione di polizia
politics la politica
poor povero
  poor quality di cattiva qualità
Pope il Papa
pop music la musica pop
pork la carne di maiale
port il porto
porter *(hotel)* il portiere
possible possibile
post *(noun)* la posta
  (verb) spedire per posta
post box la buca delle lettere
postcard la cartolina
poster il manifesto
postman il postino
post office l'ufficio postale
potato la patata
poultry il pollame
pound *(money)* la sterlina
  (weight) la libbra
powder *(cosmetic)* la cipria
pram la carrozzina
prawn il gambero
  (bigger) il gamberone
prefer preferire
prescription la ricetta
pretty *(beautiful)* grazioso, carino
  (quite) piuttosto
priest il prete
private privato
problem il problema
protection factor il fattore di
  protezione
public pubblico
pull tirare
puncture la foratura
purple viola
purse il borsellino
push spingere
pushchair il passeggino
put mettere
pyjamas il pigiama

quality la qualità
quarter il quarto
quay il molo
question la domanda
queue *(noun)* la fila
  (verb) fare la fila
quick veloce
quiet tranquillo
quite *(fairly)* abbastanza
  (fully) molto

radiator il radiatore
radio la radio
radish il ravanello
railway la ferrovia
rain la pioggia
raincoat l'impermeabile
raisins l'uvetta
rare *(uncommon)* raro
  (steak) al sangue
raspberry il lampone
rat il ratto
razor blades le lamette
read leggere
reading lamp la lampada da studio
ready pronto
rear lights i fari posteriori
receipt *(restaurants, hotels)* la ricevuta
  (shops, bars) lo scontrino
receptionist il/la receptionist
record *(music)* il disco
  (sporting etc) il record
record player il giradischi
record shop il negozio di dischi
red rosso
refreshments i rinfreschi
relax rilassarsi
religion la religione
remember ricordare
  I don't remember non ricordo
rent *(verb: flat)* affittare
reservation la prenotazione
rest *(noun: remainder)* il resto
  (verb: relax) riposarsi

restaurant il ristorante

restaurant car il vagone ristorante

return ritornare
  (give back) restituire

return ticket il biglietto di andata e ritorno

rice il riso

rich ricco

right *(correct)* giusto, esatto
  (not left) destro

ring *(noun: wedding etc)* l'anello
  (verb: phone) telefonare

ripe maturo

river il fiume

road la strada

rock *(stone)* la roccia
  (music) il rock

roll *(bread)* il panino

Roman Forum il Foro Romano

Rome Roma

roof il tetto

room la stanza
  (space) lo spazio

rope la corda

rose la rosa

round *(circular)* rotondo
  it's my round tocca a me offrire

row remare

rowing boat la barca a remi

rubber la gomma

rubbish le immondizie

ruby *(stone)* il rubino

rucksack lo zaino

rug *(mat)* il tappeto
  (blanket) il plaid

ruins le rovine, i resti

ruler *(for drawing)* la riga

rum il rum

run *(verb)* correre

sad triste

safe *(not dangerous)* sicuro

safety pin la spilla di sicurezza

St Mark's Square Piazza San Marco

St Peter's San Pietro

salad l'insalata

salami il salame

sale *(at reduced prices)* i saldi

salmon il salmone

salt il sale

same: the same dress lo stesso vestito

same again please un altro, per favore

sand la sabbia

sandals i sandali

sand dunes le dune

sandwich il panino

sanitary towels gli assorbenti (igienici)

Sardinia la Sardegna

sauce la salsa

saucepan la pentola

sauna la sauna

sausage la salsiccia

say dire
  what did you say? che cosa ha detto?
  how do you say ...? come si dice...?

scarf la sciarpa
  (head) il foulard

school la scuola

scissors le forbici

Scotland la Scozia

Scotsman lo scozzese

Scotswoman la scozzese

Scottish scozzese

screw la vite

screwdriver il cacciavite

sea il mare

seafood i frutti di mare

seat il posto

seat belt la cintura di sicurezza

second secondo

see vedere

I can't see non vedo
I see capisco
sell vendere
sellotape ® lo scotch ®
separate *(adj)* separato
separated *(couple)* separati
serious serio
serviette il tovagliolo
several diversi
sew cucire
shampoo lo shampoo
shave: to have a shave radersi
shaving foam la schiuma da barba
shawl lo scialle
she lei
sheet il lenzuolo
shell la conchiglia
shellfish *(crabs etc)* i crostacei
   (molluscs) i molluschi
sherry lo sherry
ship la nave
shirt la camicia
shoe laces i lacci per le scarpe
shoe polish il lucido per le scarpe
shoes le scarpe
shop il negozio
shopping la spesa
   to go shopping andare a fare
   acquisti
   (for food) andare a fare la spesa
short corto
shorts gli shorts
shoulder la spalla
shower la doccia
   (rain) l'acquazzone
shrimp il gamberetto
shutter *(camera)* l'otturatore
   (window) l'imposta
Sicily la Sicilia
side *(edge)* il lato
sidelights le luci di posizione
sights: the sights of ... le
   attrazioni turistiche di...
silk la seta

silver *(colour)* d'argento
   (metal) l'argento
simple semplice
sing cantare
single *(one)* solo
   (unmarried: man) celibe
   (woman) nubile
single room la camera singola
single ticket la biglietto di sola
   andata
sister la sorella
skid slittare
skiing: to go skiing andare a sciare
skin cleanser il latte detergente
ski resort la località sciistica
skirt la gonna
skis gli sci
sky il cielo
sleep *(noun)* il sonno
   (verb) dormire
sleeper *(on train)* il vagone letto
sleeping bag il sacco a pelo
sleeping pill il sonnifero
slippers le pantofole
slow lento
small piccolo
smell *(noun)* l'odore
   (verb: stink) puzzare
smile *(noun)* il sorriso
   (verb) sorridere
smoke *(noun)* il fumo
   (verb) fumare
snack lo spuntino
snorkel il respiratore a tubo
snow la neve
so: so good così bene
   not so much non così tanto
soaking solution *(for contact lenses)* il
   liquido per lenti
soap il sapone
socks i calzini
soda water l'acqua di seltz
soft lenses le lenti morbide
somebody qualcuno

somehow in qualche modo
something qualcosa
sometimes qualche volta
somewhere da qualche parte
son il figlio
song la canzone
sorry! scusi!
  I'm sorry mi dispiace
  sorry? *(pardon)* come?, scusi?
soup la zuppa
south il sud
souvenir il souvenir
spade *(shovel)* la vanga
spades *(cards)* picche
Spain la Spagna
Spanish spagnolo
spanner la chiave fissa
spares i pezzi di ricambio
spark plug la candela
speak parlare
  do you speak ...? parla...?
  I don't speak ... non parlo...
speed la velocità
spider il ragno
spinach gli spinaci
spoon il cucchiaio
spring *(mechanical)* la molla
  (season) la primavera
square *(noun: in town)* la piazza
  (adj: shape) quadrato
staircase la scala
stairs le scale
stamp il francobollo
stapler la cucitrice
star la stella
  (film) la star
start *(noun)* l'inizio
  (verb) cominciare
station la stazione
statue la statua
steak la bistecca
steal rubare
  it's been stolen è stato rubato
steamer *(boat)* la nave a vapore

  (for cooking) la pentola a pressione
stockings le calze
stomach lo stomaco
stomach ache il mal di stomaco
stop *(noun: bus)* la fermata
  dell'autobus
  (verb) fermare
  stop! alt!, fermo!
storm la tempesta
strawberry la fragola
stream il ruscello
street la strada
string *(cord)* lo spago
  (guitar etc) la corda
strong forte
student lo studente
  (female) la studentessa
stupid stupido
suburbs la periferia
sugar lo zucchero
suit *(noun)* il completo
  it suits you ti sta bene
suitcase la valigia
sun il sole
sunbathe prendere il sole
sunburn la scottatura
sunglasses gli occhiali da sole
sunny: it's sunny c'è il sole
sunshade l'ombrellone
suntan: to get a suntan abbronzarsi
suntan lotion la lozione solare
suntanned abbronzato
supermarket il supermercato
supper la cena
supplement il supplemento
sure sicuro
  are you sure? sei sicuro?
surname il cognome
sweat *(noun)* il sudore
  (verb) sudare
sweatshirt la felpa
sweet *(not sour)* dolce
  (candy) la caramella
swim *(verb)* nuotare

swimming costume il costume da bagno

swimming pool la piscina

swimming trunks il costume da bagno (per uomo)

Swiss *(man)* lo svizzero
(woman) la svizzera
(adj) svizzero

switch l'interruttore

Switzerland la Svizzera

synagogue la sinagoga

table il tavolo

tablet la compressa

take prendere

take away: to take away da portare via

take-off il decollo

talcum powder il talco

talk *(noun)* la conversazione
(verb) parlare

tall alto

tampons i tamponi

tangerine il mandarino

tap il rubinetto

tapestry l'arazzo

tea il tè

teacher l'insegnante

tea towel lo strofinaccio

telegram il telegramma

telephone *(noun)* il telefono
(verb) telefonare

telephone box la cabina telefonica

telephone call la telefonata

television la televisione

temperature la temperatura
(fever) la febbre

tent la tenda

tent pole il palo della tenda

than di

thank *(verb)* ringraziare
thank you/thanks grazie

that: that one quello
that country quel paese

that man quell'uomo
that woman quella donna
what's that? cos'è quello?
I think that ... penso che...

the *(see page 5)*

their: their room la loro stanza
their friend il loro amico
their books i loro libri
their pens le loro penne
it's theirs è loro

them: it's them sono loro
it's for them è per loro
give it to them dallo a loro

then poi, allora

there là
there is/are ... c'è/ci sono...
is/are there ...? c'è/ci sono...?

Thermos flask ® il thermos

these: these things queste cose
these boys questi ragazzi

they loro

thick spesso

thin sottile

think pensare
I think so penso di sì
I'll think about it ci penserò

third terzo

thirsty: I'm thirsty ho sete

this: this one questo
this picture questo quadro
this man quest'uomo
this woman questa donna
what's this? cos'è questo?
this is Mr ... (questo è) il signor...

those: those things quelle cose
those boys quei ragazzi

throat la gola

throat pastilles le pasticche per la gola

through attraverso

thunderstorm il temporale

Tiber il Tevere

ticket il biglietto

ticket office la biglietteria

tide la marea
tie *(noun)* la cravatta
   (verb) legare
tight *(clothes)* stretto
tights i collant
time il tempo
  what's the time? che ore sono?
timetable l'orario
tin la scatola
tin-opener l'apriscatole
tip *(money)* la mancia
  (end) la punta
tired stanco
tissues i fazzolettini di carta
to: to England in Inghilterra
  to the station alla stazione
  to the doctor dal dottore
  to the centre in centro
toast il pane tostato
tobacco il tabacco
today oggi
together insieme
toilet la toilette
toilet paper la carta igienica
tomato il pomodoro
tomato juice il succo di pomodoro
tomorrow domani
tongue la lingua
tonic l'acqua tonica
tonight stasera
too *(also)* anche
  (excessively) troppo
tooth il dente
toothache il mal di denti
toothbrush lo spazzolino da denti
toothpaste il dentifricio
torch la torcia elettrica
tour il giro
tourist il/la turista
tourist office l'ufficio turistico
towel l'asciugamano
tower la torre
  the Leaning Tower of Pisa la
  Torre di Pisa

town la città
town hall il municipio
toy il giocattolo
toy shop il negozio di giocattoli
tracksuit la tuta da ginnastica
tractor il trattore
tradition la tradizione
traffic il traffico
traffic jam l'ingorgo
traffic lights il semaforo
trailer il rimorchio
train il treno
trainers le scarpe da ginnastica
translate tradurre
translator il traduttore
  (female) la traduttrice
travel agency l'agenzia di viaggio
traveller's cheque il traveller's
  cheque
tray il vassoio
tree l'albero
trousers i pantaloni
true vero
try provare
Turin Torino
tunnel il tunnel
Tuscany la Toscana
tweezers le pinzette
typewriter la macchina da scrivere
tyre la gomma

umbrella l'ombrello
uncle lo zio
under ... sotto...
underground la metropolitana
underpants le mutande
underskirt la sottoveste
understand capire
  I don't understand non capisco
underwear la biancheria intima
university l'università
unleaded senza piombo
until fino a
unusual insolito

up su
  (upwards) verso l'alto
  up there lassù
urgent urgente
us: it's us siamo noi
  it's for us è per noi
  give it to us daccelo
use *(noun)* l'uso
  (verb) usare
  it's no use non serve a niente
useful utile
usual solito
usually di solito

vacancy *(room)* la stanza libera
vacuum flask il thermos
valley la valle
valve la valvola
vanilla la vaniglia
vase il vaso
Vatican City la Città del Vaticano
veal la carne di vitello
vegetables la verdura
vegetarian vegetariano
vehicle il veicolo
Venice Venezia
very molto
  very much moltissimo
vest la canottiera
video *(tape/film)* il video
video recorder il videoregistratore
view la vista
viewfinder il mirino
villa la villa
village il villaggio
vinegar l'aceto
violin il violino
visit *(noun)* la visita
  (verb) andare a trovare
visitor l'ospite
vitamin tablet la compressa di vitamine
vodka la vodka
voice la voce

wait aspettare
  wait! aspetta!
waiter il cameriere
  waiter! cameriere!
waiting room la sala d'attesa
waitress la cameriera
  waitress! cameriera!
Wales il Galles
walk *(noun: stroll)* la passeggiata
  (verb) camminare
  to go for a walk andare a fare una passeggiata
walkman ® il walkman ®
wall il muro
wallet il portafoglio
war la guerra
wardrobe il guardaroba
warm caldo
was: I was (io) ero
  he/she/it was (lui/lei/esso) era
washer *(for tap)* la rondella
washing powder il detersivo (per bucato)
washing-up liquid il detersivo liquido per piatti
wasp la vespa
watch *(noun)* l'orologio
  (verb) guardare
water l'acqua
waterfall la cascata
water heater lo scaldaacqua
wave *(noun)* l'onda
  (verb: with hand) salutare
wavy: wavy hair i capelli ondulati
we noi
weather il tempo
wedding il matrimonio
week la settimana
welcome benvenuto
  you're welcome di niente, prego
wellingtons gli stivali di gomma
Welsh gallese
Welshman il gallese
Welshwoman la gallese

were: you were (Lei) era
  (singular, familiar) (tu) eri
  (plural) (voi) eravate
  we were (noi) eravamo
  they were (loro) erano
west l'ovest
wet bagnato
what? cosa?
wheel la ruota
wheelchair la sedia a rotelle
when? quando?
where? dove?
whether se
which? quale?
whisky il whisky
white bianco
who? chi?
why? perchè?
wide ampio
wife la moglie
wind il vento
window la finestra
windscreen il parabrezza
wine il vino
wing l'ala
with con
without senza
woman la donna
wood *(material)* il legno
wool la lana
word la parola
work *(noun)* il lavoro
  (verb) lavorare

(machine) funzionare
worse peggiore
worst il peggiore
wrapping paper la carta da
  imballaggio
  (for presents) la carta da regalo
wrist il polso
writing paper la carta da scrivere
wrong sbagliato

year l'anno
yellow giallo
yes sì
yesterday ieri
yet ancora
  not yet non ancora
yoghurt lo yogurt
you Lei
  (singular, familiar) tu
  (plural) voi
your: your book il suo libro
  your shirt la sua camicia
  your trousers le sue scarpe
  (singular, familiar)
  your book il tuo libro
  your shirt la tua camicia
  your shoes le tue scarpe
yours: is this yours? è suo?
  (singular, familiar) è tuo?
youth hostel l'ostello della gioventù

zip la chiusura lampo
zoo lo zoo

144